I0820179

SEASONED IN APPALACHIA

Delicious Recipes from the Mountains & Hollers

Jimmy Proffitt

First published in 2025 by Rock Point, an imprint of The Quarto Group,
142 West 36th Street, 4th Floor, New York, NY 10018, USA
(212) 779-4972 www.Quarto.com

EEA Representation, WTS Tax d.o.o.,
Žanova ulica 3, 4000 Kranj, Slovenia.
www.wts-tax.si

10 9 8 7 6 5 4 3 2 1

ISBN: 978-1-57715-535-5

Digital edition published in 2025
eISBN: 978-0-7603-9664-3

Library of Congress Control Number: 2025936240

Publisher: Rage Kindelsperger
Creative Director: Laura Drew
Editorial Director: Erin Canning
Managing Editor: Cara Donaldson
Editor: Kristy Mucci
Cover and Interior Design: Lisa Berman
Photography: Abby Stewart
Food Styling: Jimmy Proffitt

Printed in Huizhou, Guangdong, China TT082025

To Mick, my husband and biggest fan.

To Lydia, the first to say I should write.

To my grandparents and my parents,
I wish I could cook you just one more meal.

To Charlie and Mary,
I'd hoe another row with you, Charlie,
and snap another mess a beans with you, Mary.

Contents

INTRODUCTION 9

WHAT IS *SEASONED IN APPALACHIA*? 11

THE SEASONS: PLANNING, PREPARATION, PLANTING, PRESERVING 15

THE APPALACHIAN KITCHEN 19

PUTTIN' UP! 25

Bread-and-Butter Pickles 26
Squash Pickles 27
Dill Pickles 28
Garden Medley Pickles 29
Green Tomato Pickles 30
Pickled Okra 31
Spicy Dilly Beans 32
Refrigerator Pickles 33

Appalachian Comforts 35

Flaky Layers Buttermilk Biscuits 38
Apple Cinnamon Biscuits 41
Drop Biscuits 42
Christmas Morning Biscuits 45
Pone Bread 46
Sausage Patties with Gravy 49
Pot Roast Gravy 50
Appalachian Chocolate Gravy 52
Pan Gravy 53
Grandmaw's Refrigerator Rolls 56
Mary's Butter Rolls 59
Brown Butter Cornbread 60
Bloody Butcher Cornbread 63
Green Tomato Onion Cornbread 64
Hot Water Cornbread 67
Fluffy Buttermilk Pancakes 68
All-Butter Pie Dough 71
Vodka Pie Dough 72
Overnight Slow Cooker Apple Butter 75
Homemade Applesauce 77
Quick Cherry Sauce 77
Grandmaw's West Virginia Hot Dog Chili Sauce 78
Spring Salad Dressing 80
Oyster Mushroom Sauce 81

Meats & Mains 83

Roast Turkey 84
Mom's Meatloaf 87
Boiled Country Ham 90
Baked Country Ham 91
Dad's BBQ Chicken 94
Sloppy Joes 97
Pennies, Dollars, and Gold Potpie 99
RB's Fish Fry and Hushpuppies 101

Salads & Sides 105

Deviled Eggs 106
Golden Potato Salad 109
Coleslaw 110
Marinated Bean Salad 113
Mick's Baked Beans 114
Appalachian Skillet Cornbread Dressing 117
Grandmaw's Baked Squash 118
Leather Britches 123

Party Foods & Beverages 125

Grandmaw's Pepperoni Rolls 128
Sausage Balls 131
Bacon Spinach Artichoke Dip 132
Cilantro Lime Chicken Wings 135
Biscuit Dough Crackers 136
Sweet Iced Tea 139
Christmas Eve Eggnog 140
Punch for 50 143
Triple-Chocolate Hot Cocoa Mix 144

Desserts & Sweets 147

World-Famous Carrot Cake 150
Zucchini Bread 153
Pineapple Upside-Down Cake 154
Mock Apple Pie 157
Green Tomato Pie 158
Appalachian Pumpkin Pie 161
Pineapple Pound Cake 162
Cranberry Orange Pound Cake 165
Christmas Crisp 166
Brownies 169
Belsnickel Cookies 172
Three-Way Shortbread 175
Mick's Banana Pudding 176
Snow Cream 179
Peanut Brittle 180
Christmas Fudge 183
Peanut Butter Fudge 184

FINAL THOUGHTS 186
ACKNOWLEDGMENTS 186
ABOUT THE AUTHOR 187
INDEX 189

Introduction

Hi, I'm Jimmy Proffitt, the fourth and youngest son of two Appalachians. I grew up in Shenandoah County in Virginia, which some don't consider to be part of Appalachia, but we have the Appalachian Trail running through the Blue Ridge Mountains to the east and the Allegheny Mountains running all the way down the western side of the state bordering West Virginia. It's all part of the Appalachian Mountain range. So, I grew up as Appalachian as anyone could have.

I was brought up learning Appalachian ways with my family and neighbors. I knew what it was to hunt, butcher, put out a garden and put it up, make or build what you need, use an outhouse and lye soap, split wood and rick it up, and to basically know how to survive on your own. These are things that I was taught by the people all around me. Of course today I don't need to do all these things, but I still do many of them. I think I got in my mother-in-law's good graces the day I helped cut wood on a chilly early fall morning and then went home and canned up the last of the beans that afternoon.

Mom grew up what I like to call Dolly Parton poor. She didn't get indoor plumbing or a TV until she got married. Her daddy was a good man with a bad history of gettin' himself in trouble. He spent many years of her childhood in jail or prison. His last big stint was because he took the blame for something he didn't do, all because he was too scared to tell my grandmaw that he was with another woman that night his brother stole something. That tells you all you need to know about Grandmaw Barton. She was a wonderful woman and dedicated to her family and her faith, but you didn't get away with much. She was incredibly talented and could make anything. I'm probably more like her than I am my parents. I don't think she ever traveled more than an hour away from home, and that's where we differ. I have a wandering spirit. I loved her deeply and miss her every day.

Dad grew up the eldest son of a preacher man. His grandparents lived in Buckhannon, West Virginia, and his parents moved into their house when they retired. Grandaddy was a Methodist minister, and a strict parent from what I hear, but I thought he was funny as I was growing up. Grandmaw had the best laugh. My favorite photo of them is one where they're both laughing and you see her beautiful smile. They were both born in West Virginia but lived on and off in Virginia too before living out their final years in Florida.

My parents and all my grandparents are now gone, so I've become the family historian. I started a blog years ago called *The Appalachian Tale* because I wanted to document who we were and what we did. What we did was eat. A lot. So my writing started to include lots of family recipes. I love to garden, something I learned from my neighbors Charlie and Mary growing up. I always say that I helped Charlie put the garden out and I helped Mary put it up. She taught me to can vegetables, make pickles, bake bread, and so much more.

I moved to Tennessee almost thirty years ago, so I've lived here over half my life. Now I'm married to a wonderful guy who supports me in all I do. We live in a little town in East Tennessee with our dogs and cats that we've rescued. I'm a freelance writer for magazines and websites in my spare time. I test family recipes I find and develop others from memory the best I can. I also have a nice little following on social media—mostly Instagram—and that led me to this cookbook. There's a story there that I tell you much later in the book. Writing a cookbook has always been a dream of mine, and now it's a reality. I hope this is the first of many, because there's so much more to my tale.

LODGE
THE APPALACHIAN TALE
Lard
Plain Flour
Self-Rising Flour
Baking Powder
Brown Sugar
Cake Flour

What Is *Seasoned in Appalachia?*

Appalachia covers the mountainous regions of thirteen states, but only one state lies entirely within its bounds, and that's West Virginia. Appalachia runs as far north as New York, then down into Pennsylvania, grabs the panhandle of Maryland, swings over into Ohio, covers half of Kentucky, picks up western and southwestern Virginia and western North Carolina, encompasses all of eastern Tennessee, swipes across parts of South Carolina and Georgia, dips down over half of Alabama, and then grabs northwestern Mississippi. We often refer to regions of Appalachia as Northern, Central, and Southern.

My book's title has a few meanings for me. First, it's about the seasons. My favorite will always be fall, followed by spring, then winter, and then summer. The seasons of the year are vitally important to Appalachia because they dictate our growing, harvesting, preserving, planning, and rest. But in Appalachia, we have over a dozen seasons, with just four of them being the big ones.

We pass time in spring with some little winters that continue to show up. It starts with Redbud Winter, which is when we get a cold spell around the time the redbud trees begin to bloom. Then we pass through Dogwood Winter. I've seen it spit snow many times on the blossoms of the dogwood tree. Not long after that is Locust Winter, and then comes Blackberry Winter. You're sure spring is here because of all the things blooming, but we're reminded by Linsey-Woolsey Britches Winter that we can't put away our warm britches just yet. And sometimes there's another cold snap that's named for the whippoorwill who begins to sing, and that can occur in between some of the other winters, or right along with one. The rest of spring is beautiful, and then summer brings the heat and humidity and with it the dog days of summer, so it's a summer within summer. We think we've gotten a break when fall is here. The colors begin to show because of cold nights and cooler days, we get a little frost, and then Second Summer gifts us with some dry weather for one last burst of warmth before winter sets in.

Seasoned in Appalachia is also about the flavors each season brings to our food. The tender greening of spring adds freshness to what we prepare, the bounty of the summer harvest brings richness and abundance, the long-tended crops of fall bring depth and warmth to the table, while winter preserves the flavors until we start all over again. In each season we may also forage for food or ingredients, for things with medicinal properties, and for things that bring beauty to our days. There is something relaxing, healing, rejuvenating, and inspiring in simply picking a wildflower to bring in and put in a vase on the windowsill, or include in a tea or a salad, or add to a tincture for a cure.

I read once that a life is to be lived in seasons, and that really resonates with me. With birth we're in our spring. We're "green" in the eyes of the world. Everything is new. We're growing and feel invincible. Then, in our twenties and thirties, we're in our summer. This is where we really begin to mature, bloom, and be fruitful. By our fifties and sixties, we enter our fall. Our colors change, and this is when we shine the best. We've fulfilled our promises and can now enjoy all that life has to offer. And, finally, in our winter, we begin to wither, lose our luster, but fully come into our wisdom. Though we seem to be in our dormancy, our families and community look to us and honor us for the legacy we're leaving for seasons to come.

And finally, it's about being well-seasoned. And I'm not talking about my cast iron. It's about a lifetime of experience. Hopefully, you'll get a sense of what it is to live an Appalachian life. And mine is not the only example; not by any means. While being Appalachian is considered almost the same thing as being Southern, it's deeper and richer than that for me, as I can identify as both. When someone asks me what makes Appalachian food or foodways different from Southern, I always say that it goes beyond the food preparation itself. It's about growing, raising, foraging, and hunting for what you eat. It's about saving the seeds, preserving the freshness of the berry, curing the meat to get you through, and planning for the next year. It involves the ingenuity, grit, and talent to provide what you need, from building a greenhouse to start your seeds to weaving a basket to gather your harvest. Preparing an Appalachian meal could be years in the making and with at least some sacrifice, knowing that it could often be about what you need more than what you want. The wants are a treat. No one needs a carrot cake, but knowing we'll want it for a special occasion means we'll grow the carrots and store them in the root cellar, saving them for such a celebration.

Appalachians are sometimes portrayed as poor because we do all these things, and while that could be the case at times, that's not unique to us, as we've all had hard times. We do these things because we're born into self-reliance, self-sufficiency, and the determination to survive on our own terms. We're not good at leaning on the shoulders of others, but we're there the moment someone needs a helping hand. Being an Appalachian is to be part of a larger family, not unlike many other cultural communities. We have a connection that goes beyond blood or region. We recognize each other. While folks in Appalachia may not put all the practices of their ancestors to use, they do use quite a few. I'm seeing homesteaders and off-gridders making a movement to live authentically, off the land, off their own resources, off their own ingenuity. That's a very Appalachian thing to do.

There are folks so seasoned in Appalachian life that they just have a knowing. The "mountain witch" or "granny witch" in Appalachian communities know each herb, root, flower, and ritual to heal anyone. They give advice on when to plant and when to harvest, tell you what dreams mean or what the future holds by reading tea leaves or bones. While it's often a woman, older and wiser, it isn't always. Men also fill that role, because traditions and practices were handed down from one generation to the next.

One of the first neighbors I remember teaching me things was MaryAnn. I helped her make lye soap many times. She only let me help prepare the washtub and set wood for the fire, and after that I was to keep my distance. Handling lye can be dangerous. So when I say I helped, it was my job to run inside and pump some water into the kettle so she could also make some coffee. Yes, her kitchen still had a well pump at the sink. You would give a couple of pumps to the handle, and then you'd hear a gurgle as air was being pushed through the pipe and the water came up and out. She was always seeing signs in things as we worked, like she knew by the way the smoke moved what the weather was gonna do. In between reading cards and leaves for folks, she made tinctures and remedies that they would buy from her.

The summer I turned thirteen, staying with my grandparents in central West Virginia, I met a blind woman who everyone went to for advice on gardening, healing, and life. She could tell you exactly when to plant your beans, corn, and potatoes by the signs. She knew every medicinal plant in the area and where it was, so she told me how to get rid of the poison ivy I got hiking through the woods. She was revered and taken care of by everyone. I was sent over to her house with a plate from the mother of a neighbor one evening. She met us at the backdoor, where she conducted most of her business, and we told her what we had and where it was on the plate for her. With the screen door closing, we got a "Thank ye."

Then there was my Grandmaw Barton, Mom's mom. She had the gift of sight. She would say all the time that she'd had a vision and then tell you what was about to happen. She even knew my granddaddy was sick before he did. She also looked for signs in things, knowing how the garden would do that spring or how hard of a winter we'd have. And she could grow anything and knew what it could be used for. I think she had more aloe vera plants than anyone needed, but we always had some she'd bottled in the medicine cabinet for cuts and burns. I got some of her gift. At times I just know things, and I too have had visions of those important events in my life.

There's lots of folklore tied to the seasons too, with little rituals that some still practice today. I remember my neighbor Mary (not be confused with my other neighbor, MaryAnn) telling me that if I got up early on the first day of spring, just as the sun came up, without speaking to anyone, I could go outside and run my hands through the dew-soaked grass and rub that dew all over my face to remove my freckles. Her sister, Clara, who was a bit of a pistol, chimed in and said if I then rubbed my hands on my butt cheeks, I'd transfer them there! I tried what they both said. It took years for my freckles to disappear.

The first of each month, the first words you're supposed to say, even before getting out of bed, are white rabbit! It brings good luck for the whole month.

The number of foggy mornings in August will forecast how many snows you'll have the following winter. Appalachians would track that to determine how much wood they needed and how much food to put up for the winter ahead. As I was working on this book, we had five foggy August mornings, so I put five beans in a jar. So far we've had two snowfalls, and this week they're calling for another. So far, we're right on track.

Grandmaw Barton

Persimmon seeds are thought to predict how hard of a winter you'll have. Wild persimmon trees are found throughout Appalachia. The fruit is small, smaller than a walnut, and when they're ripe they fall from the tree, and you pick them up rather than pick them off. Persimmon pudding is the most traditional way to use them, but you can also make bread, jelly, butter, cookies, pie, and more. They begin to ripen in late September through November and are best after the first frost. If you cut a persimmon seed open and see a spoon, it means you'll be shoveling heavy wet snow. If you see a fork, you'll have a mild winter. But if you see a knife, the weather will be severely cold, and the wind will be cutting. My aunt Alice has wild persimmons that we've harvested, so I already know what this winter holds.

If chimney smoke rises straight up, fair weather is ahead, but if it falls or curls, then rain or snow are soon to come.

Finding a four-leaf clover on Easter Sunday is thought to bring luck all year long.

A quick summer thunderstorm on a couple's wedding day is thought to bring good luck and fertility to them, but if a really bad storm sets in, then the couple will face turbulent times.

We also tell the history of our seasoned life through storytelling, poetry, and song. These heal us during heartache and hard times, celebrate the blessed moments, enrich our lives as they entertain us, and educate the generations that come after us. The song "Take Me Home, Country Roads" by John Denver in the '70s is probably the most Appalachian song that ever was. I always thought it was the story of my life with mentions of the Shenandoah River, Blue Ridge Mountains, and West Virginia.

Now get your skillet hot and set the table,

Jimmy

The Seasons

Planning, Preparation, Planting, Preserving

Winter is the season we've prepared for all year. What we do spring through fall gets us through a long, hard season. Winter is when we start planning. I've saved some seeds from the fall, and I'll inventory seeds that I had left over and try to get and store my seed potatoes before end of winter. I keep any seeds saved in envelopes in a dry, dark place. Moisture and light could cause them to sprout early. They'll keep for several years if stored properly. I've moved mostly to raised beds now, so I'll pull any weeds and add composting manure to them. I won't disturb the soil after that and hope that some snow will lie on them and get extra nitrogen and sulfur into the soil over winter. I'll also move my herbs into the greenhouse to try and overwinter them.

The first springlike day, I'm out in the sun, soaking it all in. Like much in nature, it pulls me out of hibernation. I like to feel it to my bones. The vitamin D I get from sunlight is good for my bones too. It helps our body absorb and distribute calcium to our limbs while the muscles loosen up. I itch to get out in the dirt to plant. This is when I start my seeds in the greenhouse. It really starts as winter nears its end. If you don't have a greenhouse, a warm, sunny window inside somewhere will work. You can also get some grow lights if needed. It doesn't take much room, but it does take care. I dig into a compost bin that I've been tossing kitchen scraps and grass clippings into all year. It's rich, dark soil that I amend with some peat moss, filling my seed trays. I keep a spray bottle nearby so I can mist them every day after a good watering every few days. I'll start my favorite heirloom Hillbilly tomato seeds that I saved, and a couple of other varieties, along with some cabbage, broccoli, cucumbers, squash, and okra. If any of my herbs didn't make it, I'll start some new. As soon as the last frost is past, I'll prepare the beds by turning over the soil a bit, adding any extra soil if they've compacted over the winter, and add a little fertilizer before planting anything from the greenhouse.

Summer is a season of working. I don't wish it away, but I know it's full of long, hot days, weeks of watering, and hours of harvesting, often into the dark of night to preserve my harvests. The later the sun waits to set, the more time I spend outside. It's a natural cycle that often makes me bend to its will, even when I'm tired. By late May to early June I'm starting to get some things from the garden, like green tomatoes. I can't wait for the first fried green tomato of the season! Mid-June, I'm making pickles, and we're eating squash, tomatoes, and okra every day. I'm making loaves of zucchini bread and at least one mock apple pie. As it gets deep into summer, I'm drying beans and canning peaches we get from the farmer's market. We eat fresh all summer long, and I'm sharing what we have extra of with everyone. One year we had more squash, cucumbers, and tomatoes than I had time to process, so I set up a table by the sidewalk. I left some bags and a sign that said "free." We just wanted anyone who needed it or could enjoy it to do so. One guy felt like he needed to leave an offering for us, and we got a cool vintage album.

Fall is a season to reflect, as I prepare for the next year. The tomato vines are about done, so I pull the last of the green tomatoes before the first frost and make a green tomato pie and the last batch of fried green tomatoes. I let the beans dry on the vine so they're ready to save for next year. I ripen a tomato on the windowsill so I can ferment the seeds to save, and I clip the last of the herbs I want to dry. The Leather Britches (dried green beans) are fully dry by now, and on Thanksgiving, I fix the first pot to go with dinner (page 123). I clear the garden beds of any remaining vines, roots, and weeds. I don't compost many garden plants because I don't want to reintroduce any disease that may have affected them. I'll clean up the greenhouse and all the tools, and I'll inventory them in case I need to replace anything.

Appalachia Through the Seasons

I think of myself as a storyteller above all else. I might capture a moment, record family memories, connect with other people—and I just have fun with it. Each of these poems is a bit of all that, and I hope you enjoy them. It's Appalachia through the seasons to me.

Snow Cream!

Falling and falling
Flakes from the sky
Higher and higher
They begin to lie

When accumulated
Several inches deep
Mom would grab a spoon
And hastily heap

But never should you take
From the first snowstorm
That was to cleanse the air
The wise always warned

Into the biggest bowl
Full of snow she'd fill
Along with some sugar,
Vanilla, and canned milk

Gently combining
Quickly she worked
Until the snow in the bowl
Was magically turned to dessert

How our eyes, they would beam
As we sang in a chorus
You scream, I scream
We all scream for snow cream

Pushing Through

Given from a tiny seed
Promises for another day
A want to fill a need
A will to find a way

Pushing through the ground
Sprouts fresh and green
Growing tall and proud
Determined to be seen

Budding on the bend and tip
Of each vine and branch
Nectar ready for a sip
Pollinators wait their chance

Nourished from up above
When skies fill up with gray
Followed by a warmth of love
From the sun's bright shining rays

The blossoms bear fruit
And fruit bears its bounty
It's spring's early loot
Across each hill and valley

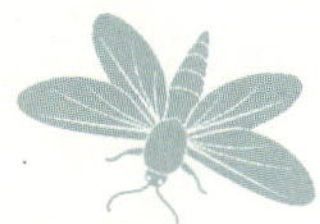

Fireflies

Flyin' 'round the yard
with their tails on fire
Hopes and wings
take 'em higher and higher

From dusk till dark
and just beyond
it's a meetin' in the field
and down by the pond

Fireflies or lightning bugs
What'er they be called
Show up each June
and they're gone by the fall

It's a wonder of nature
and magic in the same
as a beetle gets frisky
and calls with a flame

I'd go out each evening
with an old mason jar
holes in the lid
sticks and grass for its farm

One by one
gently I'd catch each blaze
put 'em inside
and set my gaze

Mesmerized by the flickers
of my bedside light
I'd watch and I'd watch
till I was out for the night

Mom would sneak in
and take 'em outside
released to the wild
on the wind they'd glide

Fireflies or lightning bugs
What'er they be called
Show up each June
and they're gone by the fall

It's a wonder of nature
and magic in the same
as a beetle gets frisky
and calls with a flame

Winding Down

Dog days now far behind
The vines begin to wither
Pick the last and dig to find
Remaining roots and gather

To the cellar and larder
Our labors lie in wait
For days are cold and harsher
inside the garden's gate

We'll save the seeds once more
That the fruit does bear
And plan our needs for next
year's score
Pushing through is life's only care

Prepare the ground and clean
the tools
For things are winding down
Inside chores now, those are
the rules
As winter's sticking 'round

E APPALACHIAN TALE
EMORIES, RECIPES, & TALES OF
AN APPALACHAIN BOY
&
LODGE
2
USA MS
GRISWOLD
ERIE PA.
GRISWOLD
ERIE
LODGE
SMITHEY
IRONWARE
COMPANY
US MADE
BROMCO

The Appalachian Kitchen

Grandmaw Barton had a pantry in the middle of the house, which, when I was a kid, looked huge. It took up every inch of space beneath the stairs and was filled with everything she needed. It held most of her canned goods but also her extra-large pots and baking pans. When you opened the door, the hinges squeaked, and all the stuff hanging on the inside of it swung back and forth. She had a room off her porch that held her freezer and more canned goods.

My cupboard, you'll find, is a small room off the kitchen that we turned into a pantry to hold all my canned goods and canning supplies. I have a baker's rack filled to the ceiling, and it holds all my large cast-iron pots, baking pans, and anything that won't fit in the kitchen. The freezer's in there, too, and by the window is where I hang my Leather Britches (page 123) to dry. On the wall in my kitchen, I have peg boards with all my cast-iron skillets, rolling pins, measuring cups and spoons, and the like, so it's right at my fingertips. In the kitchen window are herbs hanging to dry.

CUPBOARD

In my cupboards I try to keep things well-stocked, but that doesn't mean that I won't run out of something and need to find a substitute or go a little more scratch to fix what I want. Aunt Alice said that when they were growing up, whatever church Granddaddy was the minister of would have Pantry Poundings or Pound Parties for them. Parishioners would each bring a pound of something like flour, sugar, honey, salt, and lard to restock the parsonage's pantry. This might be when they first moved in, at Christmas, or when a new baby arrived. When my aunt was little, Granny came to live with them to help with the kids and the house, so she did a lot of the cooking. She probably appreciated the gifts more than anybody since she was making sure the family was fed most days.

Cast Iron

From skillets to Dutch ovens, I use cast-iron when preparing almost every meal. If you told me I could only take one thing with me to my kitchen in heaven, it would be my cast-iron skillet. You can fry with it, braise with it, bake with it, prep with it, and defend yourself with it—okay, so maybe I don't make it into heaven; I won't be too worried though, 'cause it can take the heat! But you get the idea.

I wish I had some family pieces, but growing up, my mom got rid of her cast iron when nonstick became so popular. I don't know about you, but my cast iron is more nonstick than any Teflon I've ever come across. Seasoned right, you won't have any worries about sticking. I also have lots of enameled cast iron. It's my go-to for making soups and stews, but I prefer my seasoned old cast-iron pot for making Leather Britches (page 123) at Thanksgiving and Christmas.

I have lots of new pieces, because I work with Lodge Cast Iron on projects. They're pretty good to me, sharing something new when it comes out. My aunt Alice once told me a few years ago that when she moved after retirement, she gave Granny's big 15-inch (38 cm) cast-iron skillet to the thrift store. She was afraid she couldn't use it on the new glass-top stove. My heart hurt a little hearing that, so within a week I bought my own 15-inch (38 cm) Lodge skillet. It's big, and it's heavy, but I do use it often. I don't remember Granny, but I think of her each time I pull it out. I also have several vintage pieces that I've picked up over the years. The last time I counted all my cast iron, from skillets to baking pans, it was well over fifty.

Here are some tips to care for, season, and restore your cast iron:

1 Store it in a dry place. If they can get air around them, that will help keep them from holding any moisture and will prevent rusting. That's why I hang mine on a pegboard.

2 When cleaning, I start by simply wiping it out with a dry paper towel. If it needs something more, I run it under hot water and wipe it out. If there is dried or stuck on food, a salt scrub usually does the trick. If I still feel it needs cleaning, I won't hesitate to use hot, soapy water and scrub it well. It's ok. Soap today is not as caustic as it was a hundred years ago. After cleaning, I dry it very well and wipe it down with a very thin layer of shortening. I prefer it over oil. Then I wipe it out with a clean paper towel again. If you leave too much fat in your cast iron, it can go rancid, and it can get sticky, which is the main cause of food sticking.

3 If you need to season or re-season your cast iron, first make sure it's clean and dry. Then, wipe on a thin layer of shortening. After you've given it a good coating, wipe it off with a clean, dry paper towel. You only want a matte sheen on it. Then put it in a 350°F (175°C/gas 4) oven, upside down, for 1 hour, turn it off, and let it cool completely in the oven. Repeat this three or four times for refurbished cast iron. Then the first thing you should cook in it is something you can fry with lots of oil, like chicken.

4 If you have a skillet that has buildup on it, or if you've picked one up at a yard sale or antique store, you should strip the seasoning off and start over. This can be especially important for one that you buy used, because you don't know what's been applied to it. Some resellers spray things like WD-40 on old skillets to make them look dark and seasoned. To strip it, just get a can of heavy-duty oven cleaner, spray the entire piece, and place it in a garbage bag. Set it in the sun for several hours. Then scrape off the crud and wash it. Scrub any bits still stuck, and if needed, spray it again. When it's back to raw iron, give it a vinegar bath, and clean it well with hot, soapy water, dry it completely, and re-season it.

5 If you find your cast iron has rusted, give it a bath in white vinegar for several hours. Then clean and re-season.

6 If you feel like it's beyond what you're comfortable doing to restore or re-season, there are lots of folks you can find that do it for a price. Just find someone you can verify as legitimate, especially if it is a treasured family piece or a valuable piece you've picked up.

Stoneware Bowls

I've begun a habit of collecting these. Some glazes on old pottery and stoneware contain lead, so you should pick up a simple testing kit at the hardware store to see if what you have is safe for food. If it's safe, also check for chips and cracks that food can get into. If there are no concerns, then use it to your heart's content, but always hand wash it.

Wooden Spoons and Cutting Boards

If you find old utensils at an antique store or thrift shop, you can always clean them by soaking them for a few minutes in a solution of half water and half white vinegar. Then give it a good scrub with warm, soapy water and dry right away. A salt scrub with a lemon for stubborn stuck-on messes works well. The same is true for wooden cutting boards. The one thing you never want to do is put them through the dishwasher. Wood doesn't harbor bacteria like metal or plastic can, and it won't scratch your pans. Metal can rust, and plastic can melt and peel. If you're like me and you taste your food as you cook, a wooden spoon won't burn you as quickly as a metal one will.

Bench Scraper

I have a couple in my kitchen. I always grab one when making biscuits to cut and stack the dough. They also have a measuring pattern on them, which is handy, and I prep with one too.

Biscuit Cutters

I remember my neighbor Mary had an old tuna-fish can that she used with the top and bottom cut off. I like my variety of biscuit cutters. The standards are simple and affordable, made of metal, and often come in a set. I also have some wooden ones that feel very fancy but rustic at the same time. The main thing with biscuit cutters is that you want something comfortable in your hand that cuts quickly and cleanly through the dough. What I like about the wooden ones is that I can use a little flour to clean off any biscuit dough that sticks and put it back on the shelf. After a while, they become kind of seasoned, and the dough won't stick as easily.

Wooden Rolling Pin

I have my mom's wooden rolling pin, which is now about sixty years old. It's the classic, with red handles. Just like the wooden biscuit cutters, I simply clean it with some flour if anything sticks to it. I never put it in water or use more than a damp sponge on it. The pin is incredibly smooth after all these years. Mom used it mostly for rolling out sugar cookie dough. I use it for rolling out piecrust.

Plain Flour

I typically use and refer to flour as "plain," which is also commonly known as "all-purpose." It's flour that's not had any leavening agents or seasoning added to it. If I can, I like to buy unbleached flour, which has not had any chemical whitening done to it. It has a stronger gluten structure as well, making it better for breads and baked goods.

Homemade Self-Rising Flour

There are times when self-rising flour helps to speed up the process, or you find a recipe that calls for it. To turn plain flour into self-rising, simply sift together 1½ teaspoons baking powder and ¼ teaspoon salt with 1 cup (120 g) plain flour. Use in any recipe calling for self-rising.

Cake Flour

To make cake flour, which is softer than just plain flour and makes a soft, tender crumb in cakes, you simply measure out all-purpose flour and for every cup, remove 2 tablespoons of flour and replace it with 2 tablespoons of cornstarch. Sift it well to blend it all together.

Cake Goop

I started making this Cake Goop, which is a cake release you can use in place of greasing and flouring a cake pan, a few years ago. It's shelf-stable for up to 3 months, so I make it and store it in a small mason jar. To make it, simply combine equal parts shortening, plain flour, and vegetable oil. I start by mixing the shortening and flour together until no dry flour is visible. Then I stir in the vegetable oil and mix it until it is smooth. When you use it, just brush it all over the inside of your baking pan and then pour your batter in. I love this for my Lodge cast-iron fluted pan because my cakes never stick, not even in the creases.

Homemade Baking Powder

I learned a few years ago how to make my own baking powder when I took a biscuit class from Scott Peacock. I've been making my own ever since. Commercial baking powders often add other things like cornstarch to make them last longer, and sometimes aluminum. By making your own, you not only save money; you control what's in it.

Combine two parts cream of tartar with one part baking soda. I usually measure out and use the entire container of cream of tartar that I buy and then add half as much baking soda to it. You'll need to sift it 3 or 4 times to make sure it's blended well. Then store it in an airtight container in a cool, dark place until needed. It will last you about 6 weeks. You can test to see if it's still potent by dropping a little bit in a cup of very hot water. If it fizzes, then it's still good.

Keeping and Making Brown Sugar

If you find that your brown sugar has turned hard, you can save it by placing a slice of white bread in an airtight container with the brown sugar for a few hours to overnight. It will soften the sugar, and the bread will become hard and stale. When storing brown sugar, keep it in a moist spot in the kitchen, like the cabinet near your stove, or store it in the fridge. Dry, warm spaces will only dry it out quickly.

If you find you're out of brown sugar, here's how to make your own: For each cup of white granulated sugar, add 1 tablespoon of molasses for light brown sugar and 2 tablespoons for dark brown sugar. Whisk or blend it until all the molasses is fully worked into the sugar. I start out whisking it, but then just get my hands in it to work through the lumps of molasses. It should have the consistency of damp sand when it's fully mixed.

Drying & Preserving Herbs

If you grow fresh herbs, don't let them go to waste in the fall or winter. I have my kitchen garden in pots just outside the back door. I keep rosemary, thyme, parsley, and other herbs to use fresh, but before the first frost, I cut what I can preserve to use all winter long.

I cut sprigs of herbs to make a small bundle. With kitchen string, tie the bundle together at the cut end, then use that string to hang them in a dry place, like a kitchen window that doesn't get direct sunlight, for a few weeks. When they're fully dried, you can store the leaves whole, crushed, or ground. Label them so you remember what you have. When using them in recipes calling for fresh, remember that drying concentrates the flavor, so use about a third to half of what it calls for fresh.

Basil does well chopped fresh and stuffed into ice cube trays; fill the trays with olive oil then freeze them. Store in a freezer bag. Toss a cube right into a dish while cooking or let it thaw to add to your dressing. Chives do well chopped and stored in a freezer bag just as they are. They will wilt when they thaw, so it's best to use them in cooking rather than as a topping or garnish.

Homemade Butter

I can remember learning how to churn butter in kindergarten. After visiting a farm on a field trip, our teacher put some heavy whipping cream in a mason jar and put a lid on it. Then we took turns shaking it and passing it on. After about 20 minutes, we'd made butter!

Fill a clean, quart-size (960 ml) mason jar halfway with a pint of heavy whipping cream. Put a lid on tightly and begin shaking it. After 5 minutes, you should notice that the jar is almost full of a very soft whipped cream. After 10 minutes, you should have a fully set whipped cream. You could stop here, add a little sugar and vanilla, and you would have the best whipped cream for topping a dessert or mug of hot chocolate that you've ever had. Keep shaking even though it feels like nothing is moving inside the jar. Over the next 5 minutes, you should see the whipped cream begin to break, then you'll see a lump of butter splashing around in buttermilk.

Strain the buttermilk into another jar to save. Fill a large bowl with cold water and place the lump of butter in it. Knead the butter in the cold water until the water turns cloudy. Pour it out and fill it again with clean, cold water. Repeat this 3 or 4 times until the water runs clear. Sprinkle a little salt over it and mix it in. Store it in a lidded container and refrigerate it. You can store the butter at room temperature if you're using it within an hour or so. Homemade butter could still have some of the buttermilk in it, so it is not as stable to store at room temperature for very long. If you have a butter bell, which uses a little water to seal the bell and help keep the butter cool, then you can store it at room temperature for a few days.

Rendering Your Own Lard, and What to Do with the Cracklins

When I was a kid, I went butcherin' with some neighbors on a cold November morning right after Thanksgiving. The folks we went to help made sure we understood the importance of honoring the sacrifice the hog or pig made by using every part. Rendering lard was something we did right then. There all us kids were, saddled up to a piece of plywood on a couple of sawhorses, huge knives in our hands, cutting up fat into cubes. The cubes went into a huge kettle over an open fire. It could take hours to cook them all down. When the fat melted off and the bits left were beginning to brown, they'd get squeezed in a big cast-iron press to get out any remaining liquid. The melted fat liquid was the lard that was poured into cans to store and use for months. The one thing I miss is those pressed pieces, called cracklins, that we'd have to snack on afterward. A piecrust made with lard can make one of the best pies you'll ever have. I remember Mom using a little when we made cookies, too, and she swore it made them crispier.

You don't have to process a hog or pig to make your lard, and this process is a whole lot easier now than it was when I was a kid, and you'll still get some small cracklins. They're great in cornbread, on a baked potato, or in a pan of skillet corn.

I learned this method from my friend Aliceson Bales of Bales Farms in Mosheim, Tennessee. If you're in East Tennessee, you can order some leaf lard from them. Aliceson will tell you that's the best fat to use. It's done in a slow cooker and takes most of a full day, but the cooker does the bulk of the work. You can also ask the butcher at your grocery store for fat when they trim pork. Let them know what you're using it for, and that you'd like some clean white fat (you don't want any fat that's tan or brown in appearance). It's usually just around $1 per pound, so it's very affordable. You may have to give them a day or two to get you enough, which is 4 to 6 pounds (1.8 to 2.7 kg). If the fat's got little bits of meat on it, trim off any pieces you can (leaving a little is fine). And you don't want beef fat for this; that makes tallow, which can be used for many things, but it's not for rendering lard.

If you don't have time to process it right away, store it in the freezer until you do, and then bring it out to thaw a little. When it's still slightly frozen, it's easier to cut up into small pieces. So even if you plan to render it right away, lay it out flat on a parchment-lined baking sheet and pop it in the freezer for 20 to 30 minutes to firm it up.

Set your cooker on low while you cut the fat into 1-inch (2.5 cm) cubes. Place them in the warmed slow cooker and let it cook down for 7 to 8 hours, stirring occasionally. You want to keep it on low and do this process slowly. Too high of a heat will burn your lard, and then it's not really fit to use for cooking.

When the fat has all turned to liquid and the bits in it have turned a golden brown, it's ready. Turn off the cooker and strain out the bits. Save those cracklins! They'll be small, so you won't have to press them out. The lard can be poured into sterile jars through some cheesecloth or a thin cotton towel to remove any remaining bits. I like to pour mine into wide-mouth half-pint (240 ml) or pint (480 ml) jars so I know how much I have when using it in a recipe. Put a lid on each jar, let it cool, and store it in the fridge overnight. It should be bright white when it sets. You can keep it in the fridge to use within a few months or store the jars in the freezer, where it will keep for a very long time. Just let it thaw in the fridge overnight before you're planning to use it.

Lard is perfect to fry with and to use as you would butter in baking, or to replace some of the butter, which is what Mom did when making sugar cookies. Toss a tablespoon of cracklins in cornbread batter, or in the skillet when making skillet corn, and they are wonderful. You can bake a potato by rubbing the outside of it with lard and bake it at 400°F (205°C/gas 6) for an hour, then top it with a few cracklins.

Bacon Grease

It's the frying grease of choice in our house. I can't think of a time that we were completely out and didn't have bacon to fry to have more. We keep it in a little container in the fridge, but Mom always kept it in a grease can on the back of the stove. I sometimes cook bacon in the oven, which renders even more fat from it, and then I carefully pour it off to save. I also find it's cleaner that way.

ROOT CELLAR

In the root cellar (larder) is where my childhood neighbors Mary and Charlie kept all their canned goods. The entrance was on the outside of the house. It had a huge metal door that lifted up and you walked down the stairs to a handmade wooden door into the cellar. I can still smell it. It was earthy and fresh. The coolness of it hit your nose too, especially on a hot summer day. I would take a deep breath when I stepped in.

The front half had a concrete floor and wooden shelves all down the wall. They were lined with jars full of garden things I'd helped Mary can that year. Her bread-and-butter pickles had a shelf all their own. I've got her recipe in this book (page 26). As she cooked and emptied out jars, I'd take them back down for her and store them until the next summer. She had jars that she'd used for decades. If you gave someone something you canned, it's expected that they return the jar or give something canned in exchange. Jars were and are expensive. Charlie also kept his jugs of dandelion wine behind the door. I wasn't supposed to know where it was, but then one winter, he sent me down to get a jug so he could make me a hot toddy for the bad cold I had.

The back half was still all dirt, which I think is why it wasn't musty; the dampness had somewhere to go. It was a great place for spiders too, and their webs, but I loved it—all of it! I wish I had some of Mary's canning jars to use today. In our house, we have a crawl space but no room for a root cellar. If we did, you can bet I'd set it up the same way they did.

Puttin' Up!

Puttin' Up means we're preserving food we've grown, foraged, or hunted. I helped my childhood neighbor Mary put up pickles every summer, and then we'd store it all in the root cellar, along with the root vegetables, like potatoes, that were kept down there.

Here are tips for making pickles and canned goods:

1 Use a nonaluminum pan or bowl. Aluminum is reactive and can give your pickles a metallic taste, and the acid of your vinegar can cause pitting in the aluminum.

2 Cut off the stem and bloom ends of vegetables to keep your pickles crisp and firm. You can toss the ends into your compost bin. There are enzymes in the ends that can break down the vegetable over time, so removing them helps keep your pickles crisp.

3 Always clean and sterilize your jars and lids. Give your jars a good wash in hot, soapy water and rinse them very well. You can sterilize your jars in several ways: If you have a sterilizing cycle on your dishwasher, you can use that. You can also bring a pot of water, large enough to hold your jars, to a boil, and submerge them for 10 minutes. If you're going to water-bath your pickles, you can use that pot of water. You can also sterilize them in the oven after washing, rinsing, and drying them; heat the oven to 225°F (110°C/gas ¼), lay them on their sides directly on the rack, and bake for 20 minutes. You can leave them in the oven until you're ready to fill them so the jars are tempered for the heat of the pickles.

4 Sterilize your lids and rings by boiling them in a small pot of water for 10 minutes. This will ensure your lids and rings are clean, and it will soften the rubber rings so they can form a tight seal. When placing on the rings, only tighten them finger tight. If you overtighten your rings, the lids can buckle and they may not seal. If you under-tighten them, the jar could leak during the water bath.

5 Water-bathing for canning is simply bringing a large pot of water to a rolling boil over high heat, setting your filled and sealed jars in the water, and making sure they are submerged completely with at least 1 inch (2.5 cm) of water covering them. Then let the water return to a rolling boil and hold that boil for the time noted in the recipe. If you have a way to check the temperature of the water, it should be at least 212°F (100°C), but that can vary at higher altitudes; make sure to adjust for where you live. When done, carefully remove the jars from the water and let them sit in a draft-free spot to cool slowly; this will pull the lid down for an airtight seal. Be sure to listen for the "tink" sound, and if you're in my house that's followed by me bellowing at the top of my lungs, "Sounds like pickles!" (or whatever I'm canning).

6 When using a pressure-canner, follow the directions of your canner. They can vary by brand. Most will give you guides for what to do. Pressure-canning is for nonacidic foods, like vegetables and meats. Foods preserved with an acid, such as vinegar, only need a water bath to make them shelf-stable.

7 You can reuse the rings. After opening your canned goods, use the lid only while the jar is stored in the refrigerator. Do not reuse any lids for future canning, but the rings are fine as long as they're not bent or rusted.

8 When you are making pickles, it is important to use pickling salt. Regular table salt often has iodine and noncaking agents that can make your brine cloudy and affect the taste of your pickles. Kosher and sea salts are larger, coarse salts, and using them can throw off the balance of salt in the brine, so it's best to avoid them too.

9 Cucumbers that work best for pickling are smaller, about three to six inches long, and have a thin skin that is often bumpy. The most common varieties are called pickling, Kirby, and gherkin cucumbers. You also want them to be about 2 inches (5 cm) in diameter or smaller for slices, but they can be larger for spears. English cucumbers do not make a good cooked pickle because of their very thin skin and softer flesh, but they're good for quick or refrigerator pickles.

Bread-and-Butter Pickles

This recipe is well over one hundred years old now. My neighbor Mary taught it to me. I'd help her husband, Charlie, put the garden out. Then till, weed, water, and help pick everything. In the kitchen, Mary and I made these at least once a year. When I asked her for the recipe, she made some tea. We sat down at the kitchen table, she handed me her notepad and told me to write it out, saying I'd remember it better that way, and she was right.

Each year I make my first batch mid-June, as cucumbers start coming in. I pull out the paper and hear her voice walking me through it. I still hear her laugh, because we were always laughing. Finding the funny in life is the best way to get through it. You'd think love is the best way, and it's pretty good, but funny never hurts. I loved her, and I miss her, and it hurts. Over the last thirty years, I've made probably ten times the number of pickles in my kitchen than I helped make in hers, and she's been right beside me every single time. Some people like to put the spices in cheesecloth. I like mine mixed in with the cucumbers and onions. I think they look great, and I love how the mustard seeds pop when you bite into them.

YIELD 8 or 9 pint (480 ml) jars | **SEASON MADE** Summer

About 8 pounds (3.6 kg) cucumbers, cut into ¼-inch-thick (6 mm) slices
6 medium onions, thinly sliced
⅓ cup (96 g) pickling salt
Plenty of ice
4 cups (800 g) sugar
3 cups (720 ml) white vinegar
2 teaspoons ground turmeric
2 teaspoons celery seeds
2 tablespoons mustard seeds
2 tablespoons pickling spice (usually black peppercorns, allspice, mustard seeds, etc.)

I RECKON YOU COULD
I also like to jar up any remaining pickle brine to use for cooking. You just process it with the pickles, and it's shelf-stable for a very long time. It's great for marinating chicken or pork, and I add it to my Potato Salad (page 109) and Deviled Eggs (page 106). I do the same with any pickle juice left in the jar when the pickles have been eaten.

1 In a large pan or bowl, layer the cucumber and onion slices, sprinkle with the salt and cover with a thick layer of ice. Cover with a lid and let sit for 3 hours. The salt pulls out excess moisture and the ice keeps them from breaking down and becoming soft, ensuring a crisp pickle.

2 Wash and sterilize the jars, lids, and rings and prepare a water bath (see page 25).

3 Remove any remaining ice and drain the cucumbers and onions. Fill the bowl with clean water, stir them around, and drain. Repeat two or three times. You need to rinse them multiple times to remove excess salt, which can throw off the balance of the brine.

4 In a large stockpot, add the drained cucumbers and onions, the sugar, vinegar, turmeric, celery seeds, mustard seeds, and pickling spice. Heat to boiling over high heat and cook for 5 minutes, then remove from the heat.

5 Fill each jar by carefully ladling in the hot pickles, then top with brine, leaving ½ inch (12 mm) headspace. Wipe the rims of the jars with a clean, damp cloth, removing any spillage so the jars seal properly. Put on the lids and rings, tightening by hand until just tight. Process in the boiling water bath for 10 minutes. Carefully remove the jars and let them sit in a cool, draft-free spot. You should hear them seal within a few minutes. Any that do not seal can be reprocessed: Remove and discard the lids, clean the rims again, and replace with new, unused lids. Process for 5 minutes.

6 Let the pickles sit in a cool place for at least 2 weeks before opening and serving. They need that time to pickle properly. Refrigerate after opening.

Squash Pickles

When the yellow and zucchini squash begin coming in, this is a great way to use some of them up. These are sweet and delicious, and when canned it just looks like summer.

YIELD 10 to 12 half-pint (240 ml) jars | **SEASON MADE** Summer

2½ pounds (1.1 kg) yellow squash and zucchini squash, sliced into thin rounds

2 medium yellow onions, thinly sliced

¼ cup (113 g) pickling salt

2¼ cups (450 g) sugar

2 cups (480 ml) distilled white vinegar

2 teaspoons mustard seeds

1 teaspoon ground turmeric

1 teaspoon celery seeds

1 In a large pot or bowl, add the squash and onions and cover with the salt. Let sit for 2 hours, stirring every 20 minutes. The salt will release lots of liquid from the squash, helping to ensure a crisp pickle.

2 In a 5-quart (5 L) or larger pot, add the sugar, vinegar, mustard seeds, turmeric, and celery seeds and heat to boiling over high heat. Remove from the heat. Drain the squash and onions, cover with cold water, and drain again. Repeat once more and drain to remove any excess salt. Carefully put the squash and onions into the brine and give it a light stir to coat evenly. Cover the pot and let stand for 2 hours.

3 Heat to boiling over high heat, then reduce the heat to low and simmer for 5 minutes.

4 Wash and sterilize the jars, lids, and rings and prepare a water bath (see page 25). Fill each jar by carefully ladling in the hot pickles, then top with brine, leaving ½ inch (12 mm) headspace. Wipe the rims of the jars with a clean, damp cloth, removing any spillage so the jars seal properly. Put on the lids and rings, tightening by hand until just tight. Process in the boiling water bath for 10 minutes. Carefully remove the jars and let them sit in a cool, draft-free spot. You should hear them seal within a few minutes. Any that do not seal can be reprocessed: Remove and discard the lids, clean the rims again, and replace with new, unused lids. Process for 5 minutes.

5 Let your pickles sit in a cool place for at least 2 weeks before opening and serving. They need that time to pickle properly. Refrigerate after opening.

Dill Pickles

Dill is very easy to grow in a container, and that may be best if you don't want it to take over a garden. You can save the seeds if you want from year to year. When it begins to flower, let them fully flower and turn brown. Then you can cut them and dry them out to harvest the seeds. For pickles, you want beautifully green, full fronds to place inside each jar. This recipe makes a small batch, so even if you have a lot of cucumbers coming in, you can make a variety of pickles with them, from savory to sweet.

YIELD 3 or 4 quart (960 ml) jars | **SEASON MADE** Summer

1½ cups (360 ml) white vinegar
2½ cups (600 ml) cold water
¼ cup (72 g) pickling salt
3 to 6 cucumbers, trimmed and cut into spears
2 or 3 sprigs fresh dill per jar
1 teaspoon minced garlic per jar
1 teaspoon mustard seeds per jar
½ teaspoon whole black peppercorns per jar

1 Wash and sterilize the jars, lids, and rings and prepare a water bath (see page 25).

2 In a medium saucepan, add the vinegar, water, and salt. Heat to boiling over high heat, then reduce the heat to low and simmer for 5 minutes.

3 Pack each jar tightly with spears. If the cucumbers are longer than your jar, cut them in half. Slide the dill sprigs down into the jars with the cucumbers. Top with the garlic, mustard seeds, and peppercorns. Pour the brine over them, leaving ¼ inch (6 mm) of headspace.

4 Wipe the rims of the jars with a clean, damp cloth, removing any spillage so the jars seal properly. Put on the lids and rings, tightening by hand until just tight. Process in the boiling water bath for 10 minutes. Carefully remove the jars and let them sit in a cool, draft-free spot. You should hear them seal within a few minutes. Any that do not seal can be reprocessed: Remove and discard the lids, clean the rims again, and replace with new, unused lids. Process for 5 minutes.

5 Let your pickles sit in a cool place for at least 2 weeks before opening and serving. They need that time to pickle properly. Refrigerate after opening.

Garden Medley Pickles

These are fun pickles to make because they can change depending on what you pull from the garden. I like to always have some carrots in them, though, because the carrots sweeten as they pickle and are so tasty. Spring onions are beautiful in the jars, too, and of course, you have to have cucumbers. If I have any variety of bell peppers, yellow squash, or zucchini, I'll add those, too. Just like some of these other pickle recipes, you can make as many as you like. I make these in quart jars.

YIELD 2 or 3 quart (960 ml) jars | **SEASON MADE** Summer

Vegetables

Any combination of the following to fill two or three 1-quart (960 ml) jars:

- Cucumbers
- Spring onions
- Carrots
- Any color bell pepper
- Yellow squash
- Zucchini
- Cauliflower
- Green beans

Brine

2 cups (400 g) sugar

1½ cups (360 ml) white vinegar

1 teaspoon ground turmeric

2 teaspoons mustard seeds

1 teaspoon whole black peppercorns

2 teaspoons minced garlic

1 Wash and sterilize the jars, lids, and rings and prepare a water bath (see page 25).

2 Prepare the vegetables by slicing them lengthwise into spears and sticks. Pack each jar with a variety of what you have prepared, portioning them out equally.

3 In a medium saucepan, add the sugar, vinegar, turmeric, mustard seeds, peppercorns, and garlic; heat to boiling over high heat, stirring until the sugar dissolves. Stir the brine before carefully pouring it into each jar so that the spices are present in each, leaving ½ inch (12 mm) of headspace. If you need, prepare another batch of brine to finish your jars.

4 Wipe the rims of the jars with a clean, damp cloth, removing any spillage so the jars seal properly. Put on the lids and rings, tightening by hand until just tight. Process in the boiling water bath for 10 minutes. Carefully remove the jars and let them sit in a cool, draft-free spot. You should hear them seal within a few minutes. Any that do not seal can be reprocessed: Remove and discard the lids, clean the rims again, and replace with new unused lids. Process for 5 minutes.

5 Let your pickles sit in a cool place for at least 2 weeks before opening and serving. They need that time to pickle properly. Refrigerate after opening.

Green Tomato Pickles

One year, my in-laws decided to put out 120 tomato plants because we said we wanted to freeze some tomatoes for soup and chili in the winter. It was a really good spring, and the plants were producing like crazy. My father-in-law started picking us lots of green tomatoes because I also said I loved to make fried green tomatoes. He showed up with a 5-gallon (19 L) bucket full of tiny green tomatoes. There was no way I was gonna make that many fried green tomatoes. When you're making fried green tomatoes, one large tomato will make a full batch. I told him that I could probably make something with the tiny ones, so I decided to pickle 'em. Small tomatoes are perfect for this, and for making a green tomato pie! I prefer to pickle these in half-pint (240 ml) jars.

YIELD 8 or 9 half-pint (240 ml) jars | **SEASONS MADE** Spring and fall

2 teaspoons mustard seeds
2 teaspoons pickling salt
2 teaspoons whole black peppercorns
1 teaspoon whole allspice berries
1 teaspoon whole cloves
2 cups (480 ml) white vinegar
1 cup (200 g) sugar
6 to 7 cups (2½ pounds/1.1 kg) thinly sliced green tomatoes
2 medium white onions, thinly sliced

I RECKON YOU COULD
I'm plum crazy about these on a hot dog in place of relish.

1 Sterilize the jars, lids, and rings, and prepare a water bath (see page 25). In a large pot, combine the spices and vinegar. Heat to boiling over high heat, cover, and boil for 5 minutes, then add the sugar, stirring until dissolved. Add the tomatoes and onions, reduce the heat to low, cover, and simmer for 5 minutes.

2 Fill the jars with the tomatoes and onions and top with the brine, leaving about ¼ inch (6 mm) headspace.

3 Wipe the rims of the jars with a clean, damp cloth, removing any spillage so the jars seal properly. Put on the lids and rings, tightening by hand until just tight. Process in the boiling water bath for 10 minutes. Carefully remove the jars and let them sit in a cool, draft-free spot. You should hear them seal within a few minutes. Any that do not seal can be reprocessed: Remove and discard the lids, clean the rims again, and replace with new, unused lids. Process for 5 minutes.

4 Let your pickles sit in a cool place for at least 2 weeks before opening and serving. They need that time to pickle properly. Refrigerate after opening.

Pickled Okra

For this pickling recipe, you make what you need for each jar. That makes it much easier with okra that you grow, because it doesn't all come in at once, so it's hard to make a large batch. When picking okra, you want to harvest the small tender pods; large pods are tough and mostly not edible. The small tender pods are perfect for pickling. The pickling brine is a simple salt, vinegar, and water solution that will keep in the fridge as you pick enough okra to make more jars.

YIELD 3 or 4 half-pint (240 ml) jars | **SEASON MADE** Summer

8 to 10 fresh okra pods, 2½ to 3 inches (6 to 7.5 cm) long

1 teaspoon dried dill per jar

1 teaspoon crushed red pepper or 1 to 2 whole dried red peppers per jar

2 tablespoons pickling salt

1 cup (240 ml) white vinegar

2 cups (480 ml) cold water

I RECKON YOU COULD
Pickled okra is perfect on a salad bar and fantastic in a Bloody Mary. If you want a tangy and salty appetizer, wrap whole pickled okra pods with a little prosciutto (Benton's Country Hams makes the best prosciutto), and make a honey-mustard dip for them.

1 Wash and sterilize the jars, lids, and rings and prepare a water bath (see page 25).

2 Clean the okra, pick off the leaves, and trim the stems close to the cap. Fill each jar with the dill, red pepper, and okra, packing them tightly.

3 In a 2- to 3-quart (2 to 3 L) pot, heat the salt, vinegar, and water to boiling over high heat, stirring until the salt is dissolved. Carefully fill each packed jar with the hot brine, leaving ½ inch (12 mm) headspace.

4 Wipe the rims of the jars with a clean, damp cloth, removing any spillage so the jars seal properly. Put on the lids and rings, tightening by hand until just tight. Process in the boiling water bath for 10 minutes. Carefully remove the jars and let them sit in a cool, draft-free spot. You should hear them seal within a few minutes. Any that do not seal can be reprocessed: Remove and discard the lids, clean the rims again, and replace with new, unused lids. Process for 5 minutes.

5 Let your pickles sit in a cool place for at least 2 weeks before opening and serving. They need that time to pickle properly. Refrigerate after opening.

Spicy Dilly Beans

This is a picking recipe that you make with what we call "a mess a beans"—just a good, hearty picking of green beans. We grow Tenderettes for these. They grow just the right length to fill a pint jar.

YIELD 6 to 8 pint (480 ml) jars | **SEASON MADE** Summer

2 pounds (910 g) thin, straight stringless green beans (such as Tenderette or Slenderette)

1 whole clove garlic or 1 teaspoon minced garlic per jar

1 teaspoon dried dill per jar

1 teaspoon crushed red pepper or 1 to 2 whole dried red peppers per jar

1 teaspoon mustard seeds per jar

2 tablespoons pickling salt

¼ cup (50 g) sugar

4 cups (960 ml) white vinegar

4 cups (960 ml) cold water

I RECKON YOU COULD

If you like Bloody Marys, these make a great garnish. They are also perfect cut up in a tossed salad, adding a little extra punch and texture.

1 Wash and sterilize the jars, lids, and rings and prepare a water bath (page 25). Clean and trim the green beans to fit the jars.

2 Fill each jar with the garlic, dill, red pepper, mustard seeds, and the green beans, packing them tightly with the beans standing up.

3 In a 2- to 3-quart (2 to 3 L) pot, heat the salt, sugar, vinegar, and water to boiling over high heat, stirring until the salt is dissolved. Carefully pour the brine into the packed jars.

4 Wipe the rims of the jars with a clean, damp cloth, removing any spillage so the jars seal properly. Put on the lids and rings, tightening by hand until just tight. Process in the boiling water bath for 10 minutes. Carefully remove the jars and let them sit in a cool, draft-free spot. You should hear them seal within a few minutes. Any that do not seal can be reprocessed: Remove and discard the lids, clean the rims again, and replace with new, unused lids. Process for 5 minutes.

5 Let your pickles sit in a cool place for at least 2 weeks before opening and serving. They need that time to pickle properly. Refrigerate after opening.

Refrigerator Pickles

My first try at pickles on my own were refrigerator pickles. These are a quick pickle that can be enjoyed within a few hours and up to a few weeks. Since these are for short-term storage, you just need to make sure your jar and lid are clean, but they do not need to be sterilized.

They're a salty and vinegary pickle, as opposed to a sweet pickle like bread-and-butters. The seasoning can vary, depending on what you like and have on hand. You can also make a spicy pickle by adding dried or fresh peppers to them. This recipe is for making one to two jars at a time, since they're only stored in the fridge and should be enjoyed within a few weeks. I don't recommend reusing the pickling brine for these, so make a fresh batch each time. If you want to use the brine up when the pickles are gone, try using it as a marinade for chicken or in a dressing for a salad.

YIELD 1 to 2 pint (480 ml) jars | **SEASON MADE** Summer

I RECKON YOU COULD
Other herbs and spices you can use are thyme, lemon mint, dried bay leaves, celery seeds, or whole spring onions. The combinations are endless, so let your creativity fly on these.

2 to 4 sprigs fresh dill or 1 teaspoon dried per jar
1 whole clove garlic or 1 teaspoon minced garlic per jar
1 teaspoon whole black peppercorns per jar
1 tablespoon pickling salt per jar
1 teaspoon mustard seeds per jar
1 dried or fresh hot pepper per jar (optional)
1 to 2 cucumbers, cut into ¼-inch-thick (6 mm) slices or into spears
1 cup (240 ml) white vinegar
1 cup (240 ml) cold water

To each jar, add the dill, garlic, peppercorns, salt, mustard seeds, red pepper (if using), and then fill with the cucumbers. In a large glass measuring cup, mix the vinegar and water and pour over the pickles, filling the jar. If more brine is needed, just mix equal parts vinegar and water. Put on a lid and ring, then give each jar a good shake to mix all the ingredients well. Store in the fridge for a few hours to overnight before enjoying.

Appalachian Comforts

The Best Biscuits You've Ever Made

When I was about twelve, Mary from next door showed me how to make biscuits. Hers were amazing, and since she showed me what to do, I was feeling pretty confident with my first try. My mom's best friend lived two houses down and came over on Monday evenings. They'd sit, drink coffee, and smoke cigarettes for an hour or so. I always thought of her as a really good cook. Lord knows I ate many a meal at her house.

I made my very first batch on one of those Monday evenings, so she could tell me what she thought. I thought she'd love 'em, but with one bite, she looked at me and said, "Well, they ain't bad," tossing the rest in the garbage. I didn't attempt biscuits or bread for another decade.

Since then, I've gotten my confidence back, and, well, she can kiss my biscuit! Biscuits can be intimidating because there always seems to be one person in the family that's the biscuit maker, and no one wants to challenge 'em. But most biscuit makers want to teach you. Once you have a few batches under your belt, you begin to get a feel for it. I teach kids' cooking classes, and when we get to biscuits, I tell them how Mary taught me how to make them and that she learned from her granddaddy. So, they are learning from over 150 years of experience. If that doesn't inspire you to try your hand, literally, at making biscuits, nothing will.

I think another reason biscuits scare some people is because there are so many ways to make 'em. I think I've tried them all. I've learned to make my baking powder, which is easier than you think (see page 21). Food tastes better when you get your hands into it, so I rarely use anything but my hands when I'm making a batch, and that's what I also mean by "you get a feel for it": You not only see how the dough comes together, but you can feel it.

Here are my tips for making the best biscuits you've ever had:

1 You want your ingredients cold and your oven hot. Chill your butter, flour, and bowl in the freezer. As the butter slowly melts, it creates steam that helps get more rise out of your biscuits.

2 You want your oven temp to be at 450 to 500°F (230 to 260°C/gas 8). Once you put 'em in, don't peek. Biscuits at this temp will bake in 12 to 14 minutes. You'll learn to know the smell of a biscuit when it's perfect for you.

3 When cutting in your butter, you can use a pastry blender, grate it, use a couple of knives, or simply use your fingers and pinch the butter pieces and flatten them. Pinching the butter can help make flaky layers in your biscuit where there are sheets of butter, while grating it can help make a fluffier biscuit, because the butter is distributed throughout.

4 Use full-fat buttermilk, cream, or milk. You can even make a great biscuit with just self-rising flour and heavy cream.

5 For flaky layers, you need a shaggy dough. That's a dough that seems a bit dry when you first mix all the ingredients, but as you work the dough, all the flour becomes hydrated, and the dough begins to hold together. To create the layers, you have to stack or fold your dough three to four times and roll or press out the dough in between.

6 For drop biscuits, you need a sticky dough that still allows you to handle it with floured hands on a floured surface. If it's too wet, simply add dustings of flour and gently work it in until you can handle it. These make very tender biscuits with pockets of air in them rather than layers, and they tend to take longer to bake.

7 Use a big bowl. Really big. Give yourself plenty of room to work inside the bowl. There are bowls designed specifically for biscuits, also called dough bowls, that are shallow and wide so you can get your hands in easily and work. I also have a stoneware bowl that has a flat edge on one side, making it easier to tip the bowl on its side to dump the dough out on my counter.

8 You can use a biscuit cutter, a knife, or a can, but cut straight down and back up—don't twist your cutter. Twisting your cutter or pulling a knife through the dough can bind the layers, and you won't get as much of a rise when they bake.

9 Let the biscuits touch in the pan. Each biscuit will help its neighbor rise.

10 Don't overwork your dough. It can become tough and won't be tender and flaky. When you end up with scraps, break them up and tuck them in between the biscuits. These are the baker's biscuits!

11 For over-the-top buttery biscuits, put ¼ cup (½ stick/55 g) of butter in the skillet and place it in the oven as it heats up, melting the butter and letting it brown slightly. Put the biscuits in it to bake, then, just as they come out, melt another ¼ cup (½ stick/55 g) and pour or brush it on top. The butter on the bottom will give you golden brown and crunchy bottoms, and the butter on top will be all the butter you need on your biscuit. I do this for my Flaky Layers Buttermilk Biscuits (page 38) almost every time I make them.

Flaky Layers Buttermilk Biscuits

I pay attention to all the biscuit bakers I can. I took a class years ago with Scott Peacock, and he taught me to make baking powder, which I reserve for my biscuits, and I think it makes all the difference in the world. These biscuits are perfect with just a bit of butter but are something extra special when they're doused in Chocolate Gravy (page 52).

YIELD 8 (2½-inch/6-cm) biscuits | **SEASONS ENJOYED** The Season of Life!

- 2½ cups (300 g) plain flour, plus more for dusting
- 1 tablespoon plus 1 teaspoon baking powder (see page 21)
- 1 teaspoon table salt or fine salt
- ½ cup (1 stick/115 g) salted butter, cubed and chilled
- 1 cup (240 ml) cold whole-fat buttermilk

1 Preheat the oven to 450°F (230°C/gas 8).

2 In a large bowl, mix the flour, baking powder, and salt; add the butter and toss to coat the cubes evenly. With your fingers, flatten each cube of butter (this is working flour into the butter). Continue until all the cubes are flattened out and you have sheets of butter throughout. Make a well with your hand or a spoon in the center and pour in the buttermilk. Mix until you have a shaggy, lumpy dough.

3 Dump it out onto a lightly floured surface. Gently pat it into a rectangle about 1 inch (2.5 cm) thick. At first it will still be very crumbly. With a bench scraper, cut the dough into thirds, stack the thirds, and roll or pat the stack into a rectangle about 1 inch (2.5 cm) thick. Repeat the process until the dough holds together, 3 or 4 times. When you cut it into thirds the last time, you will see the layers in the dough. Cut your biscuits into rounds or squares (see page 37 for tips).

4 Place the biscuits in a skillet or on a baking sheet with all the biscuits touching. Bake for 12 to 14 minutes, depending on how dark you like your biscuits. Serve immediately.

I RECKON YOU COULD

If you are more comfortable using a rolling pin to roll out the dough, then by all means do what you prefer. For these biscuits in particular, I like to press the dough down with my hands so I can feel it coming together. When you do use your hands, press with the center of your palm and base of your fingers, right in the middle of your hand. After a few times, you will feel how much pressure you need to use to be firm enough to work the dough while being gentle enough to not make the dough tough.

Apple Cinnamon Biscuits

I can honestly say these are award-winning! I submitted this recipe in a national contest and won first place in the baking division. For this recipe, I use baking powder and baking soda. The soda in this goes into the buttermilk rather than into the dry ingredients. The reaction of the acid in the buttermilk with the baking soda will make it foam up a bit, so use a full 1-cup (240 ml) measuring cup to mix it in. When they're done, the apples will have baked right into the biscuits.

YIELD 7 or 8 (2½-inch/6-cm) biscuits | **SEASON ENJOYED** Fall

- 1 teaspoon baking soda
- ¾ cup (180 ml) cold whole-fat buttermilk
- 2½ cups (300 g) plain flour, plus more for dusting
- 1 tablespoon baking powder
- 1 teaspoon salt
- 2 teaspoons ground cinnamon, divided
- ¼ cup (55 g) packed light brown sugar
- ½ cup (1 stick/115 g) salted butter, frozen and shredded
- 1 medium to large apple (such as Cosmic Crisp), peeled and shredded
- ¼ cup (50 g) granulated sugar
- ¼ cup (½ stick/55 g) salted butter, melted

I RECKON YOU COULD
These can also be prepared ahead of time and frozen raw. When ready to bake, place on a baking sheet and bake at 425°F (220°C/gas 7) for 25 to 30 minutes, depending on how dark you like your biscuits.

1 Preheat the oven to 425°F (220°C/gas 7).

2 In a small bowl, stir together the baking soda and the buttermilk and let sit; it will grow to about 1 cup (240 ml).

3 In a large bowl, stir together the flour, baking powder, salt, 1 teaspoon of the cinnamon, and the brown sugar. Add the shredded frozen butter and toss to mix it in. Add the shredded apple and toss to mix it in. Make a well in the center and pour in the buttermilk. Stir until you have a shaggy, lumpy dough with loose flour and bits.

4 Dump it out onto a lightly floured surface. Gently pat it into a rectangle about 1 inch (2.5 cm) thick. At first it will still be very crumbly. With a bench scraper, cut the dough into thirds, stack the thirds, and roll or pat the stack into a rectangle about 1 inch (2.5 cm) thick. Repeat the process until the dough is holding together, 3 or 4 times. When you cut it into thirds the last time, you will see the layers in the dough. Cut your biscuits into rounds or squares (see page 37 for tips).

5 Place your biscuits on a baking sheet and bake for 20 to 25 minutes, depending on how dark you like them.

6 In a small bowl, stir together the granulated sugar and the remaining 1 teaspoon cinnamon. When the biscuits are done, brush the melted butter on top and sprinkle generously with the cinnamon sugar. Serve warm.

Drop Biscuits

If biscuits scare you, drop biscuits are the way to start your biscuit journey—these are simple, use whole milk, which some call sweet milk, and have a touch of sugar in them, which helps to brown the tops. I love serving these (as pictured) with my Sausage Patties with Gravy (page 49).

YIELD 8 to 10 biscuits | **SEASONS ENJOYED** Spring, summer, fall, winter

2 cups (240 g) self-rising flour
½ teaspoon salt
1 teaspoon sugar
½ cup (1 stick/115 g) salted butter, frozen and shredded
1 cup (240 ml) cold whole milk
2 to 3 tablespoons butter, melted, for brushing on top (optional)

I RECKON YOU COULD These are great biscuits to learn with because, as you become comfortable, you can begin to play with flavor combinations by adding herbs, cheeses, and lots of other ingredients. Get creative and see what you can come up with.

1 Preheat the oven to 425°F (220°C/gas 7). Line a baking sheet with parchment paper.

2 In a large bowl, sift together the flour, salt, and sugar. Add the shredded butter and mix to distribute evenly. Make a well in the center and pour in the milk. Stir to just combine. You should have a wet, lumpy dough. If it's dry, add a little more milk.

3 Using a ¼ cup (60 ml) measuring cup or an extra-large cookie scoop, scoop the batter to make 8 to 10 biscuits, depending on how large you want them, placing them 2 inches (5 cm) apart on the prepared baking sheet.

4 Bake until browned on top, 12 to 15 minutes. Brush with some melted butter when they come out of the oven, if desired. Serve warm.

Christmas Morning Biscuits

These biscuits remind me of Christmas morning at my grandparents' house. It was at their house that I first tasted orange marmalade—the tart bits of the orange rind are replaced with the tart cranberries, but the bite and wonderful citrus flavor of the zest is in the orange sugar topping. The cinnamon butter is a nod to the cinnamon sugar reserved just for cinnamon toast. So, it's all the flavors of a special breakfast at their house rolled into one biscuit.

YIELD 8 (2½-inch/6-cm) biscuits | **SEASONS ENJOYED** Winter

Biscuits

3 cups (360 g) plain flour, plus more for dusting

1 tablespoon plus 1 teaspoon baking powder

½ teaspoon salt

1 teaspoon ground cinnamon

¼ teaspoon ground cloves

½ cup (1 stick/115 g) cold salted butter, cubed

1 medium to large apple, such as Cosmic Crisp, peeled and shredded

¾ cup (75 g) fresh or thawed frozen cranberries

1¼ cups (300 ml) whole-fat buttermilk, divided

Cranberry Glaze

¼ cup (60 ml) unsweetened cranberry juice

¼ cup (50 g) sugar

Orange Sugar

½ cup (100 g) sugar

Freshly grated zest of ½ orange

Orange Cinnamon Butter

½ cup (1 stick/115 g) salted butter, softened

¼ teaspoon ground cinnamon

1 teaspoon orange sugar

Freshly grated zest of ½ orange

1 Preheat the oven to 450°F (230°C/gas 8). Use a 10- to 12-inch (25 to 30 cm) cast-iron skillet or line a baking sheet with parchment paper.

2 Make the biscuits: In a large bowl, sift together the flour, baking powder, salt, cinnamon, and cloves. Toss in the cubed butter and pinch the pieces between your fingers, flattening them into sheets. Add the shredded apple and cranberries and mix to coat evenly. Make a well in the center and add 1 cup (240 ml) of the buttermilk, stir to combine, adding the remaining ¼ cup (60 ml) to pull it together into a slightly wet dough.

3 Dump it out onto a lightly floured surface (it will be very crumbly). Gently pat it into a rectangle about 1 inch (2.5 cm) thick. With a bench scraper, cut the dough into thirds, stack them, and roll or pat the stack into a rectangle about 1 inch (2.5 cm) thick. Repeat until the dough holds together and flaky layers appear when you cut into it, 3 or 4 times. Cut out round or square biscuits (see page 37 for tips) and place them in the skillet (or on the prepared baking sheet) so they are touching. Bake until the tops brown, 22 to 25 minutes.

4 Meanwhile, make the cranberry glaze: In a small saucepan, boil the cranberry juice and sugar over high heat, while whisking constantly, until the mixture is thick and syrupy, about 1 minute. Make the orange sugar: In a small bowl, massage together the sugar and the orange zest, using your fingers. Make the orange cinnamon butter: In a small bowl, stir together the softened butter, cinnamon, orange sugar, and orange zest.

5 When fresh out of the oven, brush the biscuits with the glaze and sprinkle on the sugar. Serve warm with the orange cinnamon butter, and have a very merry Christmas!

I RECKON YOU COULD

Start these the night before: Place the biscuits on a baking sheet, wrap tightly and refrigerate overnight. Bake them fresh and hot in the morning. You can also make the orange sugar and glaze the night before, just microwave the glaze for a few seconds to loosen it.

Pone Bread

Bread helps stretch a meal for a family, and when you want a quick bread, it doesn't get any quicker than this. It's also known as biscuit bread and skillet bread. In Appalachia, it's made for any meal, from breakfast to a late-night snack. Mick, my husband, said his mom used to make this all the time to go with dinner and they just called it wheat bread because she used wheat flour, but she and his dad both knew it as pone bread growing up.

YIELD 1 (10-inch/25-cm) loaf | **SEASONS ENJOYED** Spring, summer, fall, winter

2 tablespoons lard or shortening
2 cups (240 g) plain flour
1 tablespoon baking powder
¼ teaspoon baking soda
¼ cup (50 g) sugar
½ teaspoon salt
1 large egg
¾ cup (180 ml) buttermilk or whole milk
¼ cup (½ stick/55 g) salted butter, melted

I RECKON YOU COULD
Make some Pan Gravy (page 53) to go with this, and you're set!

1 Preheat the oven to 350°F (175°C/gas 4). Add the lard or shortening to a 10-inch (25 cm) cast-iron skillet. Let the skillet heat up in the oven to melt the fat.

2 In a medium bowl, add the flour, baking powder, baking soda, sugar, salt, egg, buttermilk or milk, and melted butter; using a spatula, stir until a wet, lumpy dough forms. If it's too dry, add a little more milk or some water.

3 When the oven has come to temperature, carefully remove the pan and pour in the batter. Smooth out the top with the spatula and bake until the top is golden and the edges are crispy and brown, 20 to 25 minutes. Slice and enjoy warm with butter, gravy, or your favorite spread. It's also great to dip in some soup or stew.

Tips for Gravy Success

Gravy is something that can be tricky to make, but once you know how to get it right, you'll find lots of uses for it and never think about store-bought versions again.

1 Melt the fat and get it hot before adding the flour. When you add the flour, sprinkle it around the pan to distribute it evenly and whisk it in quickly. Then, let the flour cook while you continue to whisk until it browns; be careful not to burn it. It should be wet; too dry at this point will just give you lumps. It's important to cook the flour to kill any bacteria that can be present in raw flour, and it removes the raw flour taste.

2 Add the liquid slowly, while whisking constantly to work out any lumps.

3 Once you have enough liquid in the gravy to make it very loose, heat it to boiling over high heat. Then the cooked flour will thicken the gravy. If it becomes too thick, simply whisk in more liquid.

4 Taste before adding salt. Some broths, especially if you use store-bought, will already be seasoned or salty. Add salt, if you feel it needs it, and any other seasonings you like.

5 If your gravy is too thin, try cooking it longer instead of adding more flour. Extra flour added at the end will likely just give you lumps and not do much to thicken the gravy. Just stir it constantly to prevent it from scorching on the bottom.

6 A basic ratio for a cup of gravy is 2 tablespoons of fat, 3 tablespoons of flour, and 1 cup (240 ml) of liquid. From there you can play with how thick or thin you want your gravy. Remember that liquids with fat in them, such as milk, will also thicken your gravy, so adjust accordingly or substitute some water for the dairy.

Sausage Patties with Gravy

Sausage gravy is something we don't have often, but it's one of my favorites. If you buy the log of ground sausage and patty it out, save the butt ends to use in the gravy. It gives you just enough to flavor it, and you still have a plate full of patties. I always warm the milk before adding it to make the gravy because cold milk will turn to steam quickly, drying out your gravy, and will make quite a mess popping all over the stove.

YIELD 2 cups (480 ml) | **SEASONS ENJOYED** Spring, summer, fall, winter

1 package (16 ounces/455 g) frozen breakfast sausage roll

2 tablespoons shortening or vegetable oil

¼ cup (30 g) plain flour

1½ to 2 cups (360 to 480 ml) lukewarm whole milk

Salt and black pepper

1 Patty out your sausage roll into 8 patties, reserving the butt ends or a couple of pieces of sausage to crumble.

2 In a large skillet over medium heat, add the shortening or oil and fry the sausage patties to render another 1 to 2 tablespoons of fat.

3 Remove the cooked patties from the skillet and add the reserved uncooked sausage. Cook it, stirring occasionally to break it up into crumbles. When the sausage is just starting to brown, increase the heat to medium-high and add the flour; whisk constantly to work it in. Continue cooking until the flour begins to brown, about 2 minutes.

4 Whisk in the warmed milk and cook, whisking constantly, until thickened the way you like it. If your gravy is too thin, don't add more flour, just let it cook a minute or two longer. If it's too thick, whisk in a little more milk. Season with salt and pepper to taste and serve warm over biscuits or toast.

I RECKON YOU COULD

If you have enough sausage fat when your sausage patties are done frying to double the recipe, then I recommend you do that. You can always freeze leftover gravy and bring it out for a fresh batch of biscuits another morning.

If you don't plan on making sausage gravy when you fry up some patties, freeze the butt ends to save for another day.

Pot Roast Gravy

Every Sunday when we were at my grandparents', Grandmaw Edge fixed a pot roast. She'd get up before sunrise and get the pot roast ready, put it in the oven, and set the timer. Then she'd peel and cube the potatoes, put them in a pot, and fill the pot with water, then set it on the back of the stove. The same would be done with some corn and whatever other vegetables we were having, but the beans would be on and at a low simmer for hours. Then she would fix us breakfast, get ready, and go hear Granddaddy preach.

As soon as we got home from church, Mom would send us to go get changed. She'd help Grandmaw check on the roast and start the potatoes. If we were having bread, which might be her refrigerator rolls (page 56), they would have been set out to rise and would be ready to go in the oven as soon as the roast came out. Then they would go get changed. We were supposed to head out and play, but I remember being in the kitchen as Grandmaw got out the hand mixer to mash the potatoes. If I was lucky, I got to taste a little bit before the beaters went into the sink. Then she'd plate the roast and pour the drippings into a pan she had getting hot on the stove so she could make the gravy. The table would be set, and we'd all sit down for Granddaddy to offer grace.

I don't know if she ever measured out anything for the gravy; she'd made it so often, she just knew what it needed. So I had to learn on my own. This is what I do, and it works for practically any kind of gravy.

YIELD 2 to 2½ cups (480 to 600 ml) gravy | **SEASONS ENJOYED** Spring, summer, fall, winter

¼ cup fat (50 g) or drippings (60 ml)

¼ cup (30 g) plain flour, plus a couple of tablespoons if needed

2 cups (480 ml) beef broth from the roast

Salt and black pepper

1 In a large skillet over medium-high heat, heat up the fat drippings until they begin to lightly sizzle. Add the flour and whisk, making sure all of the flour is mixed into the fat. If it dries out, add a little more fat while you whisk. Continue cooking until the flour begins to brown, about 2 minutes.

2 Slowly pour the broth in a steady stream while whisking constantly so lumps don't form. If your gravy is too thin, continue to cook it for a minute or two longer. If it's too thick, whisk in a little more broth or water.

3 Season with salt and pepper to taste. If you seasoned your roast, you may not need any seasoning. Serve warm.

Appalachian Chocolate Gravy

Chocolate gravy is a warm chocolate sauce that you pour over a hot biscuit. Also known as Soppin' Chocolate, it's an Appalachian tradition that is thought to have come from the Melungeon people of the Tennessee Valley; their background is multiracial with Spanish, Native American, and African ancestry. The dark cocoa is my addition because I like its richness. If you don't have dark cocoa, you can use regular unsweetened cocoa powder. It's decadent on a weekend morning, and as a treat for a special occasion, it doesn't get any better.

YIELD 2 to 2½ cups (480 to 600 ml) | **SEASONS ENJOYED** Spring, summer, fall, winter

3 tablespoons unsweetened cocoa powder
2 tablespoons unsweetened dark cocoa powder
1 cup (200 g) sugar
¼ cup (30 g) plain flour
2 cups (480 ml) whole milk
¼ cup (½ stick/55 g) salted butter

1 In a large skillet, whisk together the cocoas, sugar, and flour, making sure all lumps are broken down.

2 Over medium to medium-high heat, slowly pour in the milk while whisking; this will help prevent lumps. Continue cooking and whisking until the gravy begins to thicken, 7 to 8 minutes. Remove from the heat and stir in the butter until it's completely melted.

3 Serve warm over hot biscuits.

I RECKON YOU COULD
Serve over slices of pound cake or your favorite ice cream.

Pan Gravy

When Mom made this, she just started with some lard or shortening in a skillet and then browned some flour in it before adding water, or milk if we had it. Then she'd only season it with a little salt and pepper. For me, it tastes like home. She just called it pan gravy, so that's what I call it. We'd eat it for a snack late in the evening over slices of light bread (light bread is just white bread). I think it was a way to fill the bellies of young boys before bed on days when there wasn't much else to eat. And she would often say this was a treat her mom made when she was a little girl.

YIELD 2 to 2½ cups (480 to 600 ml) gravy | **SEASONS ENJOYED** Spring, summer, fall, winter

I RECKON YOU COULD
If we were out of lard, Mom would use shortening. It didn't have the same flavor that the lard gave it, but we ate it just the same.

¼ cup (50 g) lard
6 tablespoons plain flour
2 cups (480 ml) water or milk, or a mixture of both
Salt and black pepper

1 In a large skillet over medium-high heat, melt the lard and get it hot.

2 Add the flour and whisk, making sure all the flour is mixed in. Continue until the flour begins to brown, about 2 minutes.

3 Slowly add the water or milk while whisking constantly. Let it come back to a boil while continuing to whisk to prevent the gravy from burning. When it's thick enough, remove it from the heat, season with salt and pepper to taste, and serve over slices of light bread or pone bread.

Things to Remember When Making Bread

When they really became popular, I purchased a bread machine. I couldn't just do the basics, so I played with lots of different recipes. There are a couple of things I learned that I still do today, even when making bread from scratch.

- When making yeast breads and rolls, you can substitute potato water for all or some of the water called for in the recipe. It will make for a softer, more tender bread. And because it's adding starch, your bread can last a little bit longer. Yeast also feeds off the starch, so it helps your bread rise tall. Anytime I'm boiling potatoes and plan to just drain the water off, I drain it into another pan and let it cool. Then I give it a good stir, because the starch will settle, and portion it out into 1 or 2 cups (240 or 480 ml) in freezer bags. I freeze it until I need it for bread.
- When making yeast breads, you can substitute milk for a cup of the water it calls for. This will make your bread tender and will keep it from drying out as quickly. It also helps with gluten development. Your bread will brown a little bit more too.
- Yeast is a tricky ingredient to use. If it comes in direct contact with salt, it could kill the yeast, and it won't activate. If your water is not warm enough, it won't activate, and if it's too hot, it can kill the yeast. The ideal temperature for the water to activate yeast is around 110°F (43°C).
- You can use honey in place of sugar, but decrease the amount by a third. Since honey naturally has some antibacterial properties, it can help prevent mold, preserving your bread longer. Depending on the type of honey and how strong its flavor is, it will impart some of its flavor to the bread.

Grandmaw Edge (left), Granny (my great-grandmaw), and Aunt Gladys (aka Aunt Grandmaw), 1956

Grandmaw's Refrigerator Rolls

When we had Sunday dinner at my grandparents', there was always some sort of bread on the table. If it was rolls, it was most likely these. I found this handwritten recipe in her box, and it makes a large amount of dough. The rolls get their name because the dough sits in the fridge, and when you want to bake some, you just pull off what you want and keep the rest chilled until you need it. The longer this dough sits in the refrigerator, the more developed it becomes, making the texture of the bread very silky. It will last about seven days in the fridge. At the end of a week, I make orange rolls or cinnamon rolls, and they're so soft and tender and out-of-this-world delicious. Oh, and I make doughnuts with it, too. Aunt Alice and Uncle Jim said that Grandmaw made the best doughnuts. I've included the steps for all of these too.

My great aunt Gladys, Grandmaw's sister, also made doughnuts for us when we visited, which was only a couple of times that I can remember. What I couldn't remember was her name, so I called her Aunt Grandmaw because they looked so much alike to me. My brothers made fun, but she told me I could call her that anytime I wanted, so what did they know?

Grandmaw also made Pepperoni Rolls (page 128) with this dough, but there's more to that story in the Party Foods chapter (page 124).

YIELD 48 to 60 rolls | **SEASONS ENJOYED** Anytime I want to remember Grandmaw

2 packets (½ ounce/14 g total) active dry yeast
½ cup (120 ml) warm water (110°F/43°C)
½ cup (100 g) sugar, divided
1½ teaspoons salt
1½ cups hot water
¼ cup (50 g) shortening, softened, plus more for greasing
1 large egg, slightly beaten
6 to 6½ cups (720 to 780 g) plain flour, plus more for dusting
1 to 2 tablespoons butter, melted

1 In a large mug or 2-cup (480 ml) measuring cup, dissolve the yeast in the warm water and add 1 teaspoon of the sugar to feed the yeast. Let it sit for 5 minutes to activate. It should begin to get foamy and grow to about 1 cup (240 ml).

2 In a large bowl, stir the remaining sugar and the salt into the hot water until dissolved. Add the shortening and the beaten egg. Mix until the shortening has completely melted. Stir in the bloomed yeast. Add 4 cups (480 g) of the flour and stir until the dough is sticky and no dry flour is visible. Add additional flour, 1 cup (120 g) at a time, until the dough is smooth and easy to handle.

3 Turn the dough out onto a lightly floured surface and knead until it is smooth and elastic, about 10 minutes. Use additional flour as needed to prevent it from sticking to the surface. Using a little shortening, grease a large bowl and place the dough in it. Cover the bowl with a clean kitchen towel and let the dough rest in a warm, draft-free spot until doubled in size, 30 to 45 minutes.

4 Using shortening, grease a pan large enough to fit the number of rolls you want to make. Punch down the dough and pull out what you need, roll it into balls, and place them in the pan about 1 inch (2.5 cm) apart (at most). Cover with a clean kitchen towel and let them rest in a warm, draft-free spot until doubled in size, about 30 minutes.

5 Preheat the oven to 400°F (205°C/gas 6). Bake until well browned, 20 to 22 minutes; if they brown quickly, cover with a sheet of foil for the last 4 to 5 minutes to prevent burning. Brush the tops with a little melted butter when they come out, and let them cool for about 5 minutes before serving.

I RECKON YOU COULD

Unshaped dough can be stored in the refrigerator for up to a week. Cover well with a damp cloth and some plastic wrap to make sure the cloth stays damp so the dough doesn't dry out. Punch down and shape what you want into rolls, let rise, and bake as above. Store the remaining dough in the fridge until it is all used up.

Rolls can be frozen for later use. Place shaped dough in a greased pan and cover well with plastic wrap and freeze. When ready to use, let them thaw and rise, then bake as above.

THIS'D BE RIGHT SMART OF YA

Here are some great ways to use up the last of the dough. What I love about this is that it's flexible; make however many you can from the dough you have left. Use a loaf pan for just three to four sweet rolls, or fry up just a few doughnuts to finish it off.

To make any kind of sweet roll: Roll out the dough into a rectangle, spread on a layer of softened butter, add sugar and spices, and roll it up. Cut into individual rolls and lay them flat in a baking dish to rise before baking. Bake at 375°F (190°C/gas 5) until golden brown, about 30 minutes. Top with some icing.

To make doughnuts: Roll the dough out to about 1 inch (2.5 cm) thick. Cut into rounds or doughnuts with holes. Get a skillet hot with about 1 inch (2.5 cm) of vegetable oil in it. Working in batches, gently place each doughnut in the oil and fry for 3 to 4 minutes, then flip and fry for another 2 to 3 minutes. For cinnamon sugar doughnuts, roll them in cinnamon sugar as soon as they come out of the oil. For glazed doughnuts, drain them on a paper towel and then dip or roll them in a glaze.

Mary's Butter Rolls

I mentioned before that my neighbor Mary taught me how to make biscuits and that she learned to bake bread from her grandfather; he learned to bake bread during the Civil War when he baked for his camp. I can still see the translucent white coffee mug she used to start her yeast in. After her husband, Charlie, passed, she made them a couple of times a week. I think it kept her busy and kept people coming around. My phone would ring when she put a batch in the oven, so I knew I had about twenty minutes before I would swing by and get a fresh roll, so hot that steam would bellow out when you opened it to tuck some butter down inside. They were always so tender and delicious, practically melting in your mouth. She always used Robin Hood flour because it was a brand she found at the grocery store. I wanted to list this recipe just the way she wrote it for me, but use any flour you prefer.

YIELD 30 to 36 rolls or 2 large loaves | **SEASONS ENJOYED** Anytime I want to remember Mary

3 tablespoons salted butter, softened, plus more for greasing
2½ cups (600 ml) hot water
1 packet (¼ ounce/7 g) active dry yeast
1 teaspoon sugar
⅓ cup (80 ml) lukewarm water
6 cups (720 g) Robin Hood flour, plus more for dusting
1½ teaspoons salt

1 In a large measuring cup, melt the butter in the hot water.

2 In another large measuring cup, mix the yeast and sugar in the lukewarm water. Let it sit for 5 minutes to activate. It should begin to get foamy and grow to about 1 cup (240 ml).

3 In a large bowl, combine 5½ cups (660 g) of the flour and the salt, then make a well in the center. Pour in the hot water with the melted butter and then the activated yeast. Stir with a wooden spoon until the dough is no longer sticky and it easily pulls away from the sides of the bowl. Turn the dough out onto a lightly floured surface and knead until it is smooth and elastic, about 10 minutes. You may need to add some of the remaining ½ cup (60 g) of flour.

4 Form the dough into a ball and sprinkle a little flour around the sides of the bowl so it won't stick when it rises. Lightly grease the dough ball with a little softened butter and place it in the bowl. Cover the dough directly with a piece of wax paper and cover the bowl with a clean kitchen towel.

5 Preheat the oven to 200°F (93°C). Once it reaches full temperature, leave it for 2 minutes then turn off the heat. Set the bowl of dough in the warm oven. Let it proof and rest until doubled in size, about 30 minutes, then punch it down and grease it again. Return it to the warm oven to rest until doubled in size, about 30 minutes.

6 Adjust the oven control to 400°F (205°C/gas 6). Grease a baking pan (or pans) large enough for the number of rolls you want to make; if baking a loaf, grease a loaf pan. With well-buttered hands, pinch off pieces of dough that are slightly larger than a golf ball, roll them into balls, and arrange them in the baking pans, smooth side up, about 1 inch (2.5 cm) apart (at most). Cover with a clean kitchen towel and let them rest until doubled in size, about 20 minutes.

7 Bake for 10 minutes, then adjust the oven control to 350°F (175°C/gas 4) and bake until golden brown on top, about 15 minutes for rolls and 25 minutes for loaves. When the rolls or loaves come out of the oven, rub a little more softened butter on top. Let them cool for about 5 minutes before serving.

Brown Butter Cornbread

I reserve my 8-inch (20 cm) Lodge skillet just for this, which gives you four to six servings. Once you get your "cornbread pan" seasoned just right, you'll never have cornbread that sticks. Another way to prevent sticking is to make sure your pan is good and hot when you pour the batter in. That also gives it a nice crispy bottom. You'll notice that there's no flour in this cornbread. It doesn't need it. It bakes up tall and tender in the small pan, and the browning of the butter keeps it moist and gives it an almost movie popcorn taste as the salty flavor intensifies. When you pour the batter in, the butter envelopes the cornbread, so I like to use a baking sheet under the skillet in case any butter bubbles out while baking. You'll also see that there's a small amount of sugar in the batter, which helps brown the cornbread without making it sweet. You can double this recipe and bake it in a 10- to 12-inch (25 to 30 cm) skillet.

Note: Anytime I buy cornmeal, I like to find stone-ground unbolted. "Unbolted" means that it has not been sifted, leaving every bit of the corn in the cornmeal. I also like a coarse grind, which makes cornbread crunchier.

YIELD 4 to 6 servings | **SEASONS ENJOYED** Spring, summer, fall, winter

- ¼ cup (½ stick/55 g) salted butter
- 1 cup (138 g) plain stone-ground cornmeal
- ½ teaspoon baking powder
- ½ teaspoon baking soda
- ¼ teaspoon salt
- 1 teaspoon sugar
- 1 cup (240 ml) buttermilk
- 1 large egg, beaten

1 Preheat the oven to 425°F (220°C/gas 7).

2 Set an 8-inch (20 cm) cast-iron skillet on a baking sheet, add the butter, and place it in the oven while it preheats to melt and brown the butter. It should brown by the time the oven comes to full temperature.

3 Meanwhile, in a batter bowl, using a wooden spoon, stir together the cornmeal, baking powder, baking soda, salt, and sugar. Add the buttermilk and egg and continue mixing until completely incorporated.

4 When the butter has browned, remove the skillet from the oven and pour in the batter. Do not stir it, just let the butter come up over the batter. Bake until the cornbread is browned on top and it springs back when touched, 18 to 20 minutes.

5 Cut it into wedges in the pan or, to maintain a crispy bottom, turn it out onto a board and cut. Serve immediately.

I RECKON YOU COULD

Make this close to Thanksgiving or Christmas and freeze half a panful. Then you'll have just the right amount to use in my Appalachian Skillet Cornbread Dressing (page 117).

The perfect Appalachian summer meal includes cornbread; ripe, red, still-warm-from-the-garden tomatoes sliced thick; and green onions to dip in some salt. Finish that with a little cornbread broken up into a glass of cold buttermilk and consider yourself finner 'n frog hair, happier than a pig in mud, and fuller than a tic!

Bloody Butcher Cornbread

Bloody Butcher corn is said to have originated in the 1840s in Virginia; some stories say West Virginia, but all say it was in the central mountains of Appalachia. It's an heirloom corn that may have been cross-pollinated from corn the Native Americans grew and the corn of early European settlers. I even found one story that said it was taken by Betsey Gibson when she escaped from the Seneca tribe after being held captive for years. I wouldn't be surprised if that was the real truth, and the Europeans just claimed it as their own. If it was the Seneca, that would put the corn's origin back in West Virginia territory, which in the 1840s was still part of Virginia, since it didn't become its own state until June 20, 1863.

The corn gets its name because the red-speckled kernels resembled a butcher's bloody apron. Its flavor is a bit more earthy and nutty, which makes it perfect for making cornbread. It's also a popular corn for making moonshine. I got my bag from a distiller who likes to pass some things off to me to see what I can make. The first thing I made was cornbread. You probably won't find Bloody Butcher cornmeal at the grocery store, but a quick search will connect you to some mills that still grind it.

YIELD 4 to 6 servings | **SEASONS ENJOYED** Spring, summer, fall, winter

1½ cups (207 g) Bloody Butcher cornmeal
½ cup (60 g) plain flour
¾ teaspoon baking powder
¾ teaspoon baking soda
1 teaspoon sugar (optional)
1½ cups (360 ml) buttermilk
2 large eggs, beaten
6 tablespoons salted butter

1 In a batter bowl, use a wooden spoon to stir together the cornmeal, flour, baking powder, baking soda, salt, and sugar (if using). Add the buttermilk and eggs and mix until all the cornmeal is mixed in. It should be thick and grainy. Let the batter rest for about 10 minutes to let the cornmeal soften up a bit.

2 Preheat the oven to 425°F (220°C/gas 7). Add the butter to an 8- to 9-inch (20 to 23 cm) square pan, or a 10-inch (25 cm) skillet. Place the pan in the oven while it preheats to melt the butter.

3 When the butter has melted, remove the skillet from the oven and stir half of it into the cornbread batter, leaving the remaining half in the skillet. Transfer the batter to the hot skillet and bake until browned on top, 22 to 25 minutes. Serve it hot.

Green Tomato Onion Cornbread

This cornbread takes advantage of the abundance of green tomatoes in the spring and fall. It's a basic cornbread recipe that I dress up a little. When you turn it out, it's a showstopper with the alternating band of tomato and onion slices. You start this out on the stove while your oven preheats and you make the batter, so the tomatoes and onions begin to cook. When it's done, the onions have caramelized and the tomato slices are perfectly tender. It's like fried green tomatoes and onion rings all rolled into a pan of cornbread. It smells amazing. I prefer using bacon grease because it just adds another layer of flavor.

YIELD 8 to 10 servings | **SEASONS ENJOYED** Spring, fall

I RECKON YOU COULD
If you want to skip the green tomatoes and/or onions, you'll still have a wonderful cornbread that fills a 12-inch (30 cm) skillet to the top. You can also use this recipe to get creative and add anything you like, such as cheese, chiles, cracklins, bacon, corn—just about anything.

2 tablespoons bacon grease or vegetable oil
1 medium onion, cut into thin half-moons
1 large green tomato, sliced into ten ¼-inch-thick (6 mm) half-moons
2 cups (312 g) white or yellow plain cornmeal
1 cup (120 g) plain flour
1 tablespoon baking powder
1 teaspoon salt
2 large eggs, beaten
2 cups (480 ml) buttermilk
½ cup (1 stick/115 g) salted butter, melted

1 Preheat the oven to 425°F (220°C/gas 7).

2 As you warm up a 12-inch (30 cm) skillet over medium heat, add the bacon grease or oil; if using grease, let it melt. Carefully arrange the vegetables around the outside edge, alternating tomatoes and onions, then fill in the middle. Do not stir or flip them; just let them cook while you prepare the batter.

3 In a batter bowl, with a wooden spoon, stir together the cornmeal, flour, baking powder, and salt. Add the eggs, buttermilk, and melted butter and stir until all the cornmeal is mixed in. It should be thick and grainy. Gently pour or spoon the batter over the tomatoes and onions.

4 Bake until the cornbread is golden on top and crispy around the edges, 25 to 30 minutes. It should just begin to pull away from the pan. Let it sit for 5 minutes before turning it out. Place a platter or cutting board over the skillet and carefully flip it over to turn out the cornbread. Cut so that each slice gets a little tomato and onion, and serve warm.

Hot Water Cornbread

This is a simple fried cornbread that uses self-rising cornmeal, salt, and hot water. Depending on the coarseness of your cornmeal and how it absorbs the boiling water, it can take up to ¾ cup (180 ml) to create a soft dough that holds together. If you feel that you've added too much water, let it sit for a couple of minutes for the cornmeal to absorb it a little more. If needed, add more cornmeal, 1 teaspoon at a time.

YIELD 8 to 10 patties | **SEASONS ENJOYED** Spring, summer, fall, winter

1 cup (156 g) self-rising cornmeal
½ teaspoon salt
⅔ to ¾ cup (165 to 180 ml) boiling water
Vegetable oil

I RECKON YOU COULD
Spread just a touch of butter on each patty and serve with some warm maple syrup or honey for a nice treat or dessert. Or serve them hot and buttered with a bowl of soup beans.

1 In a medium bowl, stir together the cornmeal and salt. Pour in half of the hot water and give it a good stir. You want something closer to a dough than a batter. Add a little bit of water at a time until you have a tender dough that holds together.

2 Line a platter with paper towels. In a 10- to 12-inch (25 to 30 cm) skillet, heat about ¼ inch (6 mm) of oil over medium-high heat until it begins to shimmer, 3 to 4 minutes. Scoop out a wooden spoonful of dough and, with your hands, shape it into a patty about ½ inch (12 mm) thick. Place the patties around the skillet, leaving enough room to flip each one. Cook until the edges are firm and crispy, 3 to 4 minutes. Flip and finish cooking the other side, 2 to 3 minutes. Transfer to the prepared platter to drain before serving.

Fluffy Buttermilk Pancakes

Pancakes were something else Mom was really good at. She had a huge electric skillet, so she'd make big batches at a time. When I make them, I like to put a pat of butter in the pan just before adding the batter, like Mom did, so they get crispy, buttery edges. The trick to making them fluffy is to separate the eggs and beat the egg whites, then fold 'em back in. These are the only pancakes we make. I have a couple of old refurbished round cast-iron griddles that I like to use because I can flip the pancakes easier, but use any pan that is comfortable for you.

YIELD 6 to 10 pancakes | **SEASONS ENJOYED** Spring, summer, fall, winter

2 large eggs
1 cup (120 g) plain flour
1½ teaspoons baking powder
½ teaspoon salt
2 teaspoons sugar
1¼ cups (300 ml) buttermilk or 1 cup (240 ml) whole milk

I RECKON YOU COULD
We plum eat 'em up served warm with butter and syrup. But you could also top them with fresh fruit, whipped cream, or a dusting of powdered sugar.

1 Separate the eggs before gathering the rest of your ingredients. This gives the egg whites time to come to room temperature, so they whip easier. Reserve the yolks for the batter and place the egg whites in a deep bowl.

2 In a large bowl, add the yolks, flour, baking powder, salt, sugar, and buttermilk or whole milk. Mix with a spatula, scraping the sides and bottom of the bowl, until just combined. It does not need to be smooth.

3 Whisk the egg whites until stiff peaks form. Gently fold them into the batter. To fold, using a spatula or spoon, gently make a pass around the bowl, then go down the middle and back around the sides and down the middle again. Repeat this until no whites are visible. Do this carefully so you don't deflate the whites. The batter should be light and fluffy.

4 Get the pan hot over medium-high heat; you can use oil, butter, or keep it dry (if you have a well-seasoned pan, the pancakes won't stick). Spoon on your batter to the desired size for each pancake. Allow them to cook until bubbles begin to burst through the top, 2 to 3 minutes, then flip and allow them to cook through. Adjust your heat as needed so they don't burn. Just remember that the first pancake is always the sacrificial pancake for the cook to test!

All-Butter Pie Dough

I adapted my neighbor Mary's recipe, which called for butter-flavored shortening. I think she gave me the recipe when everyone was told to avoid real butter. I like to use salted real butter for just about everything. One of the keys is to have all your ingredients cold, just like you would for making biscuits. This will help keep the butter from melting, which can make your crust just kind of greasy and not flaky. You don't want to overwork your dough, or your crust will come out tough. Chilling it is essential so that the flour has time to hydrate. Humidity levels in the air and varying brands of flour can cause the dough to hydrate differently, so more or less water may be needed.

YIELD 2 single or 1 double piecrust | **SEASONS ENJOYED** Spring, summer, fall, winter

3 cups (360 g) plain flour, plus more for dusting

1½ teaspoons salt

1 cup (2 sticks/225 g) salted butter, frozen and shredded or chilled and cubed

½ cup (120 ml) ice water, plus a couple more tablespoons if needed

1 In a large bowl, sift together the flour and salt. If using frozen shredded butter, add it over the flour mixture and mix it in. If using chilled cubed butter, work the cubes into the flour with a pastry cutter or by hand, keeping the butter as cold as possible so it doesn't melt.

2 Add 6 tablespoons of the ice water and begin to mix to hydrate the flour. Add the remaining water, 1 tablespoon at a time, and work it into the dough until you can squeeze a lump in your hand and it holds together without sticking to your hands.

3 Dump the dough out onto a lightly floured surface and knead slightly, just until the dough comes together. Divide it into 2 equal pieces, shape each half into a disk, and wrap them in plastic and refrigerate for about 30 minutes. This will firm the butter back up and help finish hydrating the dough. You can also wrap the dough airtight and store it in the freezer for up to 3 months. Let the dough thaw overnight in the fridge.

4 When ready to make a crust, lightly flour a clean work surface and a rolling pin. Work one of the dough pieces in your hands just enough to soften and flatten it a bit. Roll out the dough, rotating a quarter turn with each pass and making sure the surface remains floured and the dough does not stick. Roll it out to ⅛ to ¼ inch (3 to 6 mm) thickness, about 1½ inches (4 cm) beyond the size of the pie dish.

5 Carefully fold the dough in half and then in half again. Place it into the pie dish and unfold. Trim the excess dough, leaving about 1 inch (2.5 cm) of overhang all around. Fold the overhang under, doubling the thickness of the crust all around the perimeter of the dish. Then crimp the edge any way you prefer. I like to pinch it between my fingers, creating a dart design. Crimping the dough down to the edge of the dish helps to keep the piecrust from shrinking as it bakes. Use the remaining dough to make a double-crust pie, if desired.

I RECKON YOU COULD

If blind-baking (par-baking or prebaking) your crust, line it with parchment and fill it with pie weights or dried beans. Bake at 375°F (190°C/gas 5) for 20 minutes to par-bake and 5 minutes more for a full bake. In Appalachia, making pie dough with lard was most common. When lard was rendered, it was often stored in the pantry in large, metal cans called "lard cans." It was also used for biscuits, breads, gravy, and frying. Making pie dough with lard gives you the flakiest crust. Lard is all fat, and butter is only about 80 percent fat. If using lard, add 2 tablespoons of flour to balance the fat, and the rest of the recipe is the same.

Vodka Pie Dough

This is not a recipe that my grandmaw or my neighbor Mary would have used; well, maybe Mary could have used a little of her husband Charlie's dandelion wine. Several years ago I started playing around with using alcohol in some of my baking; I read that it inhibits the growth of gluten. Vodka in particular doesn't leave any flavor behind in the crust, as long as you use plain, and alcohol evaporates quicker than water, so it can make for a flakier crust. Appalachians have a long history of adding alcohol to baked goods, and I've worked with local distilleries developing recipes. One year for March 14 (3/14, also known as Pi Day), I developed a recipe I called Pie Me Another Round. It used three ¼ths of alcohol from the crust through the filling to the boozy whipped cream on top. The brown sugar gives it a warm flavor and makes it perfect for a sweet pie, but you can omit the sugar if you want to use it for a savory pie.

YIELD 2 single or 1 double piecrust | **SEASONS ENJOYED** Spring, summer, fall, winter

- 2½ cups (300 g) plain flour, plus more for dusting
- 1 teaspoon salt
- 3 tablespoons packed brown sugar (optional)
- 1 cup (2 sticks/225 g) salted butter, frozen and shredded
- ¼ cup (50 ml) chilled vodka
- 4 tablespoons ice water, divided

1 In a large bowl, sift together the flour, salt, and brown sugar (if using). Add the shredded butter and toss to mix it in. Place the bowl in the freezer. Let the flour mixture chill for 30 minutes.

2 Add the chilled vodka and 2 tablespoons of the ice water to the flour and stir with a wooden spoon until a crumbly dough begins to form. Work in the remaining 2 tablespoons ice water, 1 tablespoon at a time, until it comes together. The dough is ready when you can squeeze a lump in your hand and it holds together without sticking to your hands.

3 Divide the dough in half, shape the halves into disks, and wrap them tightly in plastic wrap. Refrigerate for a minimum of 1 hour and up to overnight. This will allow the dough to completely hydrate.

4 When you're ready to make a crust, lightly flour a clean work surface and rolling pin. Work one of the dough pieces in your hands just enough to soften and flatten it a bit. Roll out the dough, rotating a quarter turn with each pass and making sure the surface remains floured and the dough does not stick. Roll out the dough to ⅛ to ¼ inch (3 to 6 mm) thickness, about 1½ inches (4 cm) beyond the size of the pie dish.

5 Carefully fold the dough in half and then in half again. Place it into the pie dish and unfold. Trim the excess dough, leaving about 1 inch (2.5 cm) of overhang all around. Fold the overhang under, doubling the thickness of the dough all around the perimeter of the dish. Then crimp the edge any way you prefer. I like to pinch it between my fingers, creating a dart design. Crimping the dough down to the edge of the dish helps to keep the piecrust from shrinking down into the pan as it bakes. Use the remaining dough to make a double-crust pie, if desired.

A Snitzing Becomes a Real Frolic!

I think every church back home had a fundraiser making apple butter in the fall. You got to know whose was the best, so you made sure to get your order in as early as possible to get a jar or two.

I was around for some apple butter makin', but I only helped stir the pot a few times. If you've ever seen it done on a large scale like that, it's pretty impressive. There's a huge copper kettle propped over a large fire. People gather to peel and cut up the apples, bushelfuls at a time. Then the sugar, water, and spices are added. It's usually stirred with a large paddle, which has to be moving at all times, scraping the bottom and all sides of the kettle once the apples begin to break down, otherwise it will scorch and ruin the whole batch. Since the fire is pretty hot, you have to stand back a bit, so the paddle is attached to a long arm. An old saying was, "Twice around the side and once down the middle, that's the way to stir the apple butter kittle!" Kittle is Appalachian for kettle.

Some paddles out there have an extra-long arm with the paddle in the middle. The arm extends way past the full width of the kettle so that two people can stir together. This was often when a young couple could meet up, spend time together talking while others are too busy to hear. So it was almost unsupervised courting, with parents just out of earshot but close enough to see what they're up to.

As a community event, it starts with a snitzing party, which is when all the apples are peeled, cored, and sliced. Then, the cooking of the apple butter is a butter-boiling or sometimes just called a frolic.

Overnight Slow Cooker Apple Butter

I make my own apple butter but don't wanna have to watch it for hours, so I simply put it in the Crockpot and go to bed. When I get up in the morning, I spend a little time finishing it and canning it up. I list Gala apples in the recipe, but I have often used a variety of apples. Some apples contain more liquid than others, so cooking time may need to be adjusted. Just cook until the apples break down and it has thickened sufficiently.

YIELD 8 to 10 half-pint (284 ml) jars | **SEASON MADE** Fall

5 pounds (2.7 kg) Gala apples, peeled, cored, and diced
1 cup (220 g) packed light brown sugar
2 cups (400 g) granulated sugar
¼ cup (60 ml) honey
½ teaspoon ground cardamom
2 teaspoons ground cinnamon
¼ teaspoon ground nutmeg
½ teaspoon ground cloves
1 teaspoon vanilla extract

1 In a large slow cooker, add the apples, brown sugar, granulated sugar, honey, cardamom, cinnamon, nutmeg, cloves, and vanilla. Cook on high for 1 hour, then reduce the heat to low and cook overnight for 6 to 8 hours. Or, if you have time that day, you can leave it on high and cook for 5 to 6 hours, stirring occasionally as they cook. When they are done, the apples will have cooked down to small, tender chunks and the liquid will be thick enough to coat the back of a spoon.

2 Using an immersion blender, puree the cooked-down apples right in the pot until thick, but not completely smooth. You want some texture to it. If you use a regular blender, work in batches, being careful handling the warm apple butter.

3 Sterilize the jars, bands, and lids and prepare a water bath (see page 25).

4 Fill the jars with the apple butter, leaving about ¼ inch (6 mm) headspace. Wipe the rims of the jars with a clean, damp cloth, removing any spillage so the jars seal properly. Put on the lids and rings, tightening by hand until just tight. Process in the boiling water bath for 10 minutes. Carefully remove the jars and let them sit in a cool, draft-free spot. You should hear them seal within a few minutes. Any that do not seal can be reprocessed: Remove and discard the lids, clean the rims again, and replace with new, unused lids. Process for 5 minutes. Refrigerate after opening.

Homemade Applesauce

Similar to making apple butter, but this is much quicker and made on the stovetop.

YIELD 5 ½ to 6 cups (1.3 to 1.4 L) | **SEASON ENJOYED** Fall

I RECKON YOU COULD
If you like it a bit sweeter, increase the amount of sugar up to ½ cup (100 g). You can substitute light brown sugar for a little richer flavor. You can also sweeten it with about ¼ cup (60 ml) honey and increase it to taste.

5 to 6 large apples (about 3 pounds), peeled, cored, and cut into 1-inch (2.5 cm) cubes

⅓ cup (65 g) sugar

¼ teaspoon salt

1 tablespoon apple cider vinegar

1 In a large saucepan, bring the apples, sugar, salt, vinegar, and ⅓ cup (80 ml) of water to a boil over high heat. Cover the saucepan, reduce the heat to low, and simmer until the apples are tender and begin to fall apart, 25 to 30 minutes. Let cool for 10 minutes.

2 Using a hand mixer or a blender, puree the mixture just long enough to make it as smooth as you like.

3 Let cool completely. In a container of your choice, refrigerate for up to 1 week or freeze for up to 6 months. If freezing, leave ½ inch (12 mm) of headspace in the container to give room for it to expand.

Quick Cherry Sauce

I keep bing cherries in the freezer all year long. I buy them fresh and pit them myself. Frozen cherries soften quickly and release some liquid, so you get a nice sauce with tender cherries. This sauce is great to spoon over a cheesecake, pound cake, or ice cream.

YIELD 5 ½ to 6 cups (1.3 to 1.4 L) | **SEASON ENJOYED** Fall

1½ cups (235 g) frozen bing cherries

¼ cup (50 g) sugar

2 tablespoons cornstarch

¼ teaspoon almond extract

Pinch of freshly grated nutmeg

In a small saucepan, bring the cherries, sugar, cornstarch, almond extract, and nutmeg to a boil over medium-high heat. Reduce the heat to medium and cook, stirring constantly to prevent it from scorching, until lightly thickened, about 5 minutes. Remove from the heat and let it cool before serving. Enjoy just warm or completely cool, depending on how thick you like it (it gets thicker as it cools). Store in an airtight container in the fridge for up to 1 week.

Grandmaw's West Virginia Hot Dog Chili Sauce

Hot dog chili sauce is something of a West Virginia staple, and a West Virginia chili dog is not just a staple, it's an institution. The warm sauce is just the start. For the full experience, you'll also add Coleslaw (page 110), mustard, and some chopped raw onion on top. When I was going through Aunt Alice's collection of recipe cards that Grandmaw had, I came across this recipe. Alice said it was the best, and I have to agree. As a matter of fact, I never enjoyed a chili dog before this. When I make it, I prefer a canned tomato sauce that is simply made with tomatoes and a little bit of seasoning like garlic and onion. I don't recommend any with herbs like basil or oregano.

YIELD 6 to 7 cups (1.4 to 1.7 L) | **SEASONS ENJOYED** Spring, summer, fall, winter

2 pounds (907 g) ground beef, somewhat lean but not over 85%
2 large onions, diced (about 4 cups/500 g)
1 large bell pepper, diced
1 clove garlic, minced
2 teaspoons salt
¼ cup (32 g) chili powder
2 teaspoons ground cumin
3 tablespoons plain flour
1½ cups (360 ml) beef broth
2 cups (480 ml) tomato sauce

1 In a 4- to 5-quart (4 to 5 L) stockpot over medium heat, add the ground beef, onions, pepper, and garlic and cook, stirring occasionally, until lightly browned, breaking up the beef as it cooks so that no clumps remain.

2 In a small bowl, stir together the salt, chili powder, cumin, and flour. Sprinkle the mixture over the meat, coating it evenly. Stir in the broth and tomato sauce.

3 Reduce the heat to low and simmer, uncovered, for 1 hour and 30 minutes. Keep an eye on it and stir it every few minutes. If it tries to stick, reduce the heat further. When it's done, it should be thick enough to heap on a spoon without running off. Serve warm.

I RECKON YOU COULD

When I make it, I freeze some in 1-cup (240 ml) portions, and when we get a hankerin' for it, we grill some hot dogs, thaw some sauce out, and have it warmed up in a matter of minutes.

Spring Salad Dressing

This is a family favorite that's been passed down through my uncle's side. They've been dressing fresh spring vegetables from the garden with it for generations. It's nice and creamy and a great alternative to ranch dressing. You can make this in a mason jar and give it a good shake before serving. It's a great base if you want to add a few more things like garlic, or fresh or dried herbs.

YIELD 1¼ cups (300 ml) | **SEASONS ENJOYED** Spring, summer

1 cup (240 ml) mayonnaise
1 tablespoon sugar
2 tablespoons whole milk
2 tablespoons apple cider vinegar
Salt and black pepper

To a pint-size (480 ml) mason jar, add the mayonnaise, sugar, milk, vinegar, and a dash of salt and pepper; put a lid on it, and give it a good shake to combine everything well. This will keep for up to 1 week in the fridge and can be served directly from the jar.

Aunt Alice, Dad's youngest sister, married Andy in 1971. This dressing comes from his family.

Left to right, front: Ricky, Pat, Bobby, and me. Middle: Grandmaw, Uncle David, Aunt Alice. Back: Grandaddy, Dad, and Mom.

Oyster Mushroom Sauce

My mother-in-law keeps an eye out for me to find oyster mushrooms growing in her backyard. There are a couple of roots that have grown through the ground under the shade of her mulberry tree, so I can count on those for a nice little harvest in the spring, sometimes in the summer, and again in the fall or a mild winter. Our neighbors Charlie and Mary went mushroom hunting often, and Mary would make a simple mushroom gravy to go over chicken-fried steak. I didn't get her recipe, but I know she made it with evaporated milk, and even though she called it gravy, I don't remember it having any flour. I thought I'd try my hand at this sauce; it's great over beef or chicken. If I'm making a beef dish, I'll use beef broth and I use chicken broth for chicken breasts or thighs. Like Mary, I also save any broth from cooking, so sometimes it will have a layer of fat on top that I can use to sauté the mushrooms. The splash of bourbon adds a little extra flavor and is completely optional. That's my addition, not Mary's!

YIELD 1½ cups (360 ml) | **SEASONS ENJOYED** Spring, fall

I RECKON YOU COULD
If you can't forage for oyster mushrooms, you can sometimes find them packaged fresh in the grocery store and also packaged dried. If you use the dried, simply follow the instructions on the package to rehydrate them.

2 tablespoons salted butter, beef fat, or chicken fat

Up to 1 cup (70 g) roughly chopped wild oyster mushrooms

1 can (12 ounces/354 ml) evaporated milk

½ cup (120 ml) beef or chicken broth

Salt and black pepper

A splash of bourbon (optional)

1 In a large cast-iron skillet over medium-high heat, melt the butter or fat; add the mushrooms and cook, stirring occasionally, until tender, 5 to 6 minutes.

2 Add the evaporated milk and broth and reduce the heat to medium. Bring to a heavy simmer and cook, stirring occasionally, to reduce the sauce to the thickness you prefer. Reducing it by half will take 10 to 12 minutes.

3 Season with salt and pepper to taste and, if desired, add a splash of bourbon at the end for extra flavor.

Meats & Mains

Roast Turkey

I didn't roast my first turkey until I was probably twenty-five years old and had moved out on my own. It was something I had to learn, and from what everyone says after cleaning their plate, I'm pretty good at it.

Remember, frozen turkeys take a long time to thaw. I get mine out of the freezer and into the fridge on the Saturday before Thanksgiving. Then I like to brine it overnight in salt water with a few spices. I probably do this because our neighbor Mary always did; a carryover of preparing a wild turkey, which can be pretty gamy, and her husband, Charlie, always hunted their turkey. So, if you prefer to skip this step, you can, but it does add flavor and helps keep it moist.

I have a huge stockpot that can fit a whole turkey, so it rests in that the night before. I keep it on the back porch; where we live it gets down into the low forties at night around Thanksgiving, so it's pretty safe. I don't do stuffing in my bird. I make a cornbread dressing and, instead, I fill the turkey with apple, carrots, celery, onions, and rosemary or other fresh herbs I still have on hand.

YIELD 1 Turkey | **SEASONS ENJOYED** Fall, winter

1½ cups (434 g) pickling salt
½ cup (110 g) packed brown sugar
1 tablespoon whole black peppercorns
2 tablespoons dried thyme
4 bay leaves
1 whole turkey, thawed
¼ cup (½ stick/55 g) salted butter, softened
Salt and black pepper
1 large apple, cut into wedges
3 to 4 medium-small whole carrots
2 to 3 ribs celery
1 medium sweet yellow onion, quartered
3 or 4 sprigs any fresh herbs you like (such as rosemary, thyme, and sage)

I RECKON YOU SHOULD
Plan on 1 pound (454 g) per person when buying a turkey

1 In a medium saucepan, heat the salt, sugar, peppercorns, thyme, bay leaves, and about 4 cups (960 ml) of water to boiling over high heat; stir until the salt and sugar dissolve. Remove from the heat.

2 To a large pot or bucket, add the turkey, the mixture, and enough water to completely cover the bird. Cover and refrigerate (or store somewhere cold) overnight or up to a full day.

3 Preheat the oven to 325°F (165°C/gas 3). Remove the turkey from the brine and pat it dry with paper towels. Place it in a roasting pan, breast side up.

4 Rub the softened butter all over the turkey and under the breast skin, then sprinkle with salt and pepper. Stuff the cavity with the apple, carrot, celery, onions, and fresh herbs. Tuck the wings under and tie the legs together with kitchen twine. Add enough water to completely cover the bottom of the pan. Loosely tent with foil, making sure it doesn't touch the top of the turkey, and roast, 14 minutes per pound. After 40 minutes, carefully pull back the foil tent and baste the bird. Put the tent back and continue roasting, basting every 20 minutes.

5 In the last 30 minutes, remove the foil to let the skin brown. You can increase the temperature a bit, up to 425°F (220°C/gas 7), to brown it a little quicker. The turkey is done when a meat thermometer inserted in the deepest part of the breast and thigh reads 160 to 170°F (71 to 77°C). A 10- to 12-pound (4.5 to 5.4 kg) turkey will take about 2½ to 3 hours. Let the turkey rest for 10 minutes before carving.

Mom's Meatloaf

Mom and Dad, June 8, 1963

We had a set of blue-and-white Pyrex mixing bowls that I think Mom and Dad got as a wedding present. When she got out the biggest bowl in the set, I knew she was about to make her meatloaf. When it came time to start mixing, she always used her hands, and I always wanted to help. So she'd have me wash all the way up to my elbows, and I'd stand on a kitchen chair at the counter and dig in. I remember she would pick up the whole mound all at once and the bowl would stick and then drop back on the counter with a bang as she transferred it to the baking dish. Then she'd shape it, leaving room all around the sides so any grease that might build up had a place to go and she could spoon it off. Then, with her largest serving spoon, she would spread on the ketchup topping as it got close to being done. While it was in the oven finishing, she'd get out the box of instant mashed potatoes and open a can of peas. That's just how it was: a little homemade, a little not. When I make it, I make real mashed potatoes. I don't think I've made instant since leaving home.

YIELD 8 servings | **SEASONS ENJOYED** Spring, summer, fall, winter

I RECKON YOU COULD

If my mom was out of bread crumbs or crackers, she'd use quick-cooking oats instead.

Leftover meatloaf makes the best sandwich ever—yes, I said ever. All you need is two slices of light bread with mayonnaise on them. I advise adding any additional ketchup topping you can steal from the pan.

Meatloaf

2 pounds (907 g) lean ground beef

1½ cups (168 g) plain bread crumbs or 1 sleeve saltine crackers, crushed

¾ cup (180 ml) milk

1 large egg

¼ cup (60 ml) ketchup

2 tablespoons yellow mustard

2 tablespoons barbecue sauce

2 tablespoons Worcestershire sauce

1 teaspoon salt

½ teaspoon black pepper

1 small white or yellow onion, diced (1 cup/125 g)

1 tablespoon minced garlic

1 can (6 ounces/170 g) tomato paste

Ketchup Topping

½ cup (120 ml) ketchup

1 tablespoon apple cider vinegar

¼ cup (55 g) packed brown sugar

1 Preheat the oven to 375°F (190°C/gas 5).

2 Make the meatloaf: In a large bowl, break up the ground beef. In a small bowl, stir together the bread crumbs, milk, and egg until the bread crumbs are moistened; add to the ground beef and, using your hands, mix well. Add the ketchup, mustard, barbecue sauce, Worcestershire sauce, salt, pepper, onions, garlic, and tomato paste. Using your hands, mix until well combined and it holds together.

3 Transfer the mixture to a casserole dish, free-form it into a round or oblong loaf about 3 inches (7.5 cm) high, and bake until it's brown on top, about 50 minutes.

4 Meanwhile, make the ketchup topping: In a small bowl, stir together the ketchup, vinegar, and brown sugar.

5 Brush the ketchup topping on the meatloaf, then continue baking until the glaze is bubbly and beginning to brown and it reaches an internal temperature of 160°F (71°C), about 20 minutes.

6 Let the meatloaf rest for 10 minutes before serving so it will firm up and hold together better.

Cooking a Country Ham

Some folks refer to the building or shed out behind their house as the smokehouse. My in-laws still do, but I don't know how many folks are smoking meat at home these days. Our neighbors Charlie and Mary had a smokehouse that turned into more of a workshop for Charlie. There was a big chest freezer out there, and occasionally a smoked ham would be hanging. When you walked in, it still smelled a bit smoky, and you could see the darkened beams from all the smoke it once held. There was even a pit in the floor where the fire was kept, with a drain so he could wash it out. Mary tried to pretty it up with some curtains at the window. There was a single light bulb hanging from the ceiling that I think Charlie put in when they got the freezer.

It had been years since they had smoked anything out there, but he did have a working smokehouse further up in the yard, across from the garden. You would never suspect he was smoking meats up there, though, because it was their old outhouse! He had moved it from where it sat for the first few decades that they lived in the house. They had added a bathroom, so it became obsolete. As Appalachians often do, they found uses for everything. He used an old stockpot in the seat to build a fire to smoke his own jerky. Having a properly cured country ham hanging up that you shaved some meat off of was pretty common. Charlie did that so often there was a knife hanging from the ceiling next to it.

To cook a country ham, you need to soak it for one to two days to remove some of the salt and soften up the meat. Then you can boil it or bake it, or a combination of both. It's easy to do, but because it's so time-consuming, it's mostly reserved for special occasions. Here's what some folks back home did. The boiling method was generally for serving cold for sandwiches later or to fry up for breakfast or dinner. The roasting method is generally for serving warm from the oven as the main for a holiday meal.

Great-Granddaddy, Henry Patrick Cockran, by the hog pin. He was gone long before I was born, and this is the only picture I've ever seen of him.

Boiled Country Ham

Boiling a country ham is perfect when you simply want ham to serve cold or sliced and fried up for breakfast or dinner. Sliced thin on a fresh hot biscuit with a little sorghum and butter is my favorite! To reheat a slice in a cast-iron skillet, start with a little bit of bacon grease or lard and fry it just a couple of minutes on each side or until it begins to brown.

YIELD 25 to 30 Servings | **SEASON ENJOYED** Winter

1 country ham (15 pounds/6.8 kg)
1 cup (220 g) packed brown sugar
½ cup (120 ml) apple cider vinegar
½ cup (120 ml) blackstrap molasses
2 to 3 quarts (1.9 to 2.8 L) boiling water

I RECKON YOU SHOULD
Plan on ¼ to ⅓ pound (113 to 151 g) per serving

1 Clean your ham by scrubbing any mold off the outside under running water.

2 In a stockpot or lard can large enough to hold the whole ham, put the cleaned ham inside, and add the brown sugar, vinegar, and molasses. Add the boiling water; the entire ham should be covered. Cover the pot and let it sit at room temperature overnight.

3 The next morning, remove the ham and rinse it off well. Rinse the stockpot, return the ham to the pot, and fill it with enough fresh water to completely cover the ham.

4 Heat to boiling over high heat, then reduce the heat to medium-low, so the water is at a low boil, and cook until the hock-end of the bone is loose and you can pull it out, about 5 hours or 20 minutes per pound. It should reach an internal temperature of 165°F (73°C).

5 Let sit in that water until cool enough to handle, 2 to 3 hours.

6 Transfer the ham to a large cutting board, cut off the layer of fat and discard, slice the ham into serving-size portions, and refrigerate it. Slices can be served warm or cold. To warm, fry it in a skillet until seared on each side or in the oven at 325°F (165°C/gas 3) for just a few minutes.

Baked Country Ham

We love to bake a country ham for the holidays. Taking something as "country" as can be and dressing it up quite a bit! It's so tender and flavorful, with just a hint of holiday spice. It also makes the most amazing presentation when you bring it to the table. And leftovers never last long.

YIELD 25 to 30 Servings | **SEASON ENJOYED** Winter

1 country ham (15 pounds/6.8 kg)
2 cups (440 g) packed brown sugar, divided
2 cups (480 ml) regular or spiced apple cider, divided
½ cup (120 ml) molasses
2 to 3 quarts (1.9 to 2.8 L) boiling water
Whole cloves, for decorating
Orange slices, for decorating

I RECKON YOU SHOULD
Plan on ¼ to ⅓ pound (113 to 151 g) per serving

1 Clean your ham by scrubbing any mold off the outside under running water.

2 In a stockpot or lard can large enough to hold the whole ham, put the cleaned ham inside, add 1 cup (220 g) of the brown sugar, 1 cup (240 ml) of the apple cider, and the molasses. Add the boiling water; the entire ham should be covered. Cover the pot and let it sit at room temperature overnight.

3 The next morning, remove the ham and rinse it off well. Rinse the stockpot, return the ham to the pot, and fill it with enough fresh water to completely cover the ham; soak for an additional night.

4 Preheat the oven to 325°F (165°C/gas 3).

5 Transfer the ham to a large roasting pan, skin side up, and add 4 to 5 cups (1 to 1.2 L) of water. If you want additional flavor, replace some of the water with apple juice or apple cider. Cover it with foil and bake for about 5 hours, or 20 minutes per pound.

6 Meanwhile, in a small pot over medium heat, simmer the remaining 1 cup (240 ml) of apple cider, and the remaining 1 cup (220 g) of brown sugar, stirring occasionally, until reduced by half.

7 At the beginning of the fourth hour, transfer the roasting pan to a heatproof surface, keeping the ham in the pan. Using a sharp knife, cut off the layer of fat, leaving ¼ to ½ inch (6 to 12 mm) of fat over the ham. Score the remaining fat in a crosshatch pattern and stud the ham with whole cloves if desired.

8 Return the ham to the oven, uncovered, and bake until the shank bone is loose and the internal temperature reaches 165°F (73°C), 45 minutes to 1 hour, basting with the glaze every 15 minutes. Let the ham rest for about 15 minutes before serving whole, on a large carving board, decorated with orange slices (if desired), for a showstopper. Carve slices about ¼ inch (6 mm) thick for serving warm. Refrigerate any leftovers.

Dad at the Toms Brook Volunteer Fire Department, 1998

Shenandoah Valley BBQ Chicken

In the Shenandoah Valley, there's a barbecue chicken recipe that most everyone's had. I grew up eating it for lunch or dinner on many Saturdays throughout the spring, summer, and fall. My dad used to help make it at the Toms Brook fire hall for fundraisers, where he was a volunteer fireman. They'd have the Annual Fireman's Parade every August, followed by the lawn party. As kids, we ran around the fire hall all the time, but on the weekend of the parade, we'd be there from early morning till late into the night.

On Friday night, folks from all over the county would line up as the fire trucks from each town came down Main Street. The kids would be right at the front so we could all catch the candy and whatnot that they'd throw from the trucks. Our pockets would be filled with candy, and we would hold a fistful or two as we walked around, shoving pieces of bubblegum into our mouths trying to see who could blow the biggest bubble. When that wad lost its flavor, we'd start all over again.

After the parade, everyone would head to the side and back lawns of the fire hall. Booths and tents were set up with games for us to play. Mom would save dimes so we could try our hand at the dime toss. Even though we were kids, it was thrilling to get one to land on a plate or in a cup that we could win, but the goal was to get it to land on the very top where there was money to be won. I don't remember winning any, but I'm pretty sure one of my brothers walked away with some money, only to spend it in another booth. The ring toss was another of our favorites, as was the legendary dunking booth. I wasn't as good at throwing the ball as my older brothers were, but when Dad ended up in the booth, I think we all got a good shot in!

The big deal for me at the lawn party though was the barbecue chicken. Every fire hall, Ruritan club, school, and church had, and probably still does have, a firepit out back. Not the kind you line your chairs around for a nice little fire to toast marshmallows. These were at least twenty feet (6 m) long and made of cinderblocks stacked two to two and a half feet (0.6 to 0.7 m) high with large grates that covered the top. Inside the pit, fires would run the whole length, chicken halves would line the grates, and the cooking would begin.

Mopping sauce, named so because it's applied like you're mopping the floor, was made by the gallons and slathered all over the chicken every 20 or 30 minutes as chicken was flipped: An empty grate would be placed over a grate full of chicken and then flipped and put back on the fire. Then the top grate was moved down to cover the next full grate and flipped again, continuing one after the other, moving the whole feast three feet (0.9 m) in either direction. A grate full of chicken halves could weigh fifty or sixty pounds (23 or 27 kg), so it took two men with thick gloves working in unison to flip them, while someone came from behind with a mop, which was just a towel held by tongs that they dipped in a bucket of sauce. It was a continuous operation and after about two hours, the chicken, a little charred in spots but glistening, would come off and then be dipped in a little fresh sauce and slipped into a foil-lined white bag. It would continue to steam in the bag, so it was always tender and juicy. You'd rip open the bag and commence digging in. I remember my fingers being black from the char on the end of the chicken leg and wing. The mopping sauce is vinegar-based and had a tang to it that was intoxicating to me.

Toms Brook Volunteer Fire Department has been hosting the parade and lawn party for more than seventy-five years. I would guess that my dad was part of it for well over half of those years. He passed in 2010 and had been a volunteer since he was a kid. When I was growing up, if he wasn't working, he was at the fire hall or the church.

Dad and his best friend also barbecued many weekends for the church. They would start early in the morning so the chicken would be ready by 11 a.m., and they continued until it sold out—and it always sold out. Folks would line up in their cars down the road, waiting up to an hour. I remember coolers packed with bulging white bags ready to sell. They would fill the grates again and again, cooking round after round. Sometimes Mom would help collect the money, and when she wasn't counting back change, she had one chicken she was working on and one in our own cooler to take home for later. We may have been their best customers.

I never thought to ask Dad for the recipe; he never made it at home that I can remember. It's possible he only knew the recipe for making gallons of the sauce at a time. I started researching it many years ago and realized this style of barbecue was a tradition throughout the whole valley and not just where my dad helped out. It seems a man in Montezuma, just outside Dayton, Virginia, was credited with first developing the sauce in the 1950s. My grandaddy was a preacher and served in Dayton for a few years right after my parents married. I don't know if Dad learned it from his dad or if the recipe was shared from one community event and fundraiser to another. I do know that each group that made it would add their secret, but the real secret was in the coming together as a community. When you make it on the scale like at church or the fire hall, it takes a whole community, and that makes all the difference.

Dad's BBQ Chicken

I've worked on this barbecue recipe for years, so mine is a little different too, and I've adapted it for my charcoal grill. I can't get it a couple of feet from the coals like with those enormous firepits, but I can raise it up a bit. I keep a hot side and a cold side of the grill to still allow for a two-hour grilling time. I think that's important because something this good shouldn't be rushed.

YIELD 6 servings | **SEASONS ENJOYED** Spring, summer, fall

1 cup (240 ml) vegetable oil
2 cups (480 ml) apple cider vinegar
½ cup (120 ml) Worcestershire sauce
Juice of 1 lemon
2 tablespoons salt
2 teaspoons garlic powder
2 teaspoons poultry seasoning
1 teaspoon black pepper
¼ cup (60 ml) honey
4 to 6 chicken leg quarters or 2 to 4 chicken halves (I prefer the leg quarters)

I RECKON YOU COULD
It's always served as half a chicken back home, but leg quarters are easier to get at the grocery store. I have a notion to serve it warm with Coleslaw (page 110), "roast'nears" (my mom's dialect for grilled corn on the cob), and a hot cheesy biscuit.

1 In a medium bowl, whisk together the oil, vinegar, Worcestershire sauce, lemon juice, salt, garlic powder, poultry seasoning, pepper, and honey; this is the mopping sauce.

2 Place the chicken pieces in a large resealable plastic bag, add 1 cup (240 ml) of the mopping sauce, making sure the pieces are evenly coated. Seal the bag, and let it marinate in the refrigerator for 2 to 4 hours, or overnight for best results. Divide the remaining sauce between two containers and store in the refrigerator.

3 When you are ready to begin barbecuin', prepare a charcoal grill by setting the grate on the highest level and the coals on one side of the grill, to make a hot and cold side.

4 When the coals are ready, place the marinated chicken pieces on the cold side of the grill, dispose of the used marinade, and close the lid. Grill for 45 minutes to 1 hour, rotating and turning the chicken pieces every 10 to 15 minutes and basting with one of the containers of the reserved mopping sauce.

5 Move the chicken to the hot side of the grill and continue cooking for 1 hour to 1 hour and 15 minutes or until the internal temperature reaches 160°F (71°C), turning and basting it every 8 to 10 minutes. If it begins to burn, move the chicken to the middle of the grill, keeping it closer to the coals; you want it over the direct heat as much as possible to make sure it cooks through, but you don't want to char it too much.

6 Transfer the cooked chicken pieces to a roasting pan with a lid. Warm the last container of sauce in the microwave or on the stove and transfer to a large bowl and dip each piece of chicken in the sauce to baste it once more. Wrap each piece in foil and put them back in the roasting pan, cover with the lid, and let them steam for 20 to 30 minutes while the rest of the meal is prepared. For an authentic experience, serve each piece warm in the foil, where it catches the juices to dip bites of the chicken in as you enjoy it.

Sloppy Joes

Sloppy Joes was one of my all-time favorite meals growing up. We had it often in school, and Mom would make it every now and again, but it was always canned, and I can't say that it liked me as much as I liked it. A few years ago, we grew lots of bell peppers in every color we could find, and I really got a chance to perfect my recipe for Sloppy Joes. You can certainly use green peppers, but I like how much color the red and yellow peppers give it. Those, or even orange peppers, are also a little sweeter. It's way easier than you think to make, and it tastes so much better. The Worcestershire sauce and brown sugar are what give it that unmistakable Sloppy Joe flavor.

YIELD 8 to 10 servings | **SEASONS ENJOYED** Summer, fall

2 pounds (907 g) ground beef
2 tablespoons extra-virgin olive oil
1 large yellow bell pepper, diced
1 large red bell pepper, diced
1 medium sweet yellow onion, diced
1 tablespoon minced garlic
1 can (28 ounces/794 g) tomato puree or 4 to 5 cups (720 to 900 g) chopped fresh tomatoes cooked down and pureed
2 tablespoons Worcestershire sauce
¼ cup (55 g) packed brown sugar
½ teaspoon salt
½ teaspoon black pepper
1 can (6 ounces/170 g) tomato paste
8 to 10 buns, for serving

1 In a large skillet over medium heat, cook the ground beef, breaking it up so there are no clumps, until cooked but not browned, about 10 minutes. Drain off the excess fat.

2 In a large stockpot or Dutch oven, heat the olive oil over medium heat, add the peppers and onions and cook, stirring occasionally, until the onions become a little translucent and the peppers are tender, 10 to 12 minutes. In the last 1 to 2 minutes, stir in the garlic.

3 Add the ground meat, pureed tomatoes, Worcestershire sauce, brown sugar, salt, pepper, and tomato paste and reduce the heat to medium-low. Cook, stirring frequently, until thickened, 15 to 20 minutes.

4 Serve on large buns. I like to toast the buns so they hold together a little better.

Pennies, Dollars, and Gold Potpie

Appalachians are steeped in tradition, superstition, and ritual. I call this Pennies, Dollars, and Gold Potpie and make it for New Year's Day, because it represents all the symbols that are thought to bring good luck, good fortune, wealth, and health for the year ahead.

The pennies are the black-eyed peas, because they represent good luck and good fortune. The dollars come from the collard greens, because anything green represents the money that you want to bring into your life. The gold is found in the gold potatoes, corn, and cornbread topping, so make sure you use yellow cornmeal; that's very important, to bring not just money, but wealth. I use pork because pigs root forward to find food and you want to move forward. Avoid chicken, and chicken broth, because they have to scratch for their food, and the last thing you want to do is to scratch for every morsel in the year ahead. It's all prepared in a cast-iron skillet, which I think adds a fourth important element, and that's a fortitude of steel to face the new year!

YIELD Yield: 4 to 6 servings | **SEASONS ENJOYED** New Year's Day, winter

Potpie Filling

2 strips bacon

¾ to 1 pound (340 to 454 g) pork loin, cut into ½-inch (12 mm) cubes

2 tablespoons plain flour

1 cup (130 g) diced carrots

1 cup (120 g) diced celery

1 cup (140 g) diced Yukon Gold potatoes

1½ cups (195 g) frozen corn kernels or 1 can (15 ounces/425 g) corn kernels, drained

1½ cups (195 g) frozen black-eyed peas

1½ cups (130 g) frozen chopped collard greens

1 teaspoon dried or 2 teaspoons fresh parsley

1 teaspoon dried or fresh rosemary

½ teaspoon dried or 1 teaspoon fresh thyme

¼ teaspoon dried chives or ½ teaspoon fresh chives

2 bay leaves

½ teaspoon salt

¼ teaspoon black pepper

1 cup (240 ml) heavy cream

Cornbread Crust

1 cup (156 g) yellow self-rising cornmeal

1 cup (240 ml) buttermilk

1 large egg

¼ cup (½ stick/55 g) browned butter (see Tip on following page)

1 Make the filling: In a 12-inch (30 cm) or larger cast-iron skillet, cook the bacon strips over medium heat to slowly crisp them and render as much grease as possible. Remove the bacon when crisp.

2 Add the pork loin and cook, stirring occasionally, until it begins to brown, about 10 minutes. Sprinkle the flour over the pork and stir with a spatula until the flour browns, about 1 to 2 minutes. Add the carrots, celery, potatoes, corn, black-eyed peas, collard greens, parsley, rosemary, thyme, chives, bay leaves, salt, and pepper. Crumble the bacon strips into the skillet and add 2 cups (480 ml) water. Stir gently. Cover and reduce the heat to medium-low. Simmer until the potatoes and carrots begin to soften, about 10 to 15 minutes.

continued on following page

continued from previous page

3 Add the heavy cream and simmer, uncovered, for 5 minutes, stirring constantly to make sure nothing sticks while it thickens up.

4 Preheat the oven to 425°F (220°C/gas 7).

5 Make the cornbread crust: In a batter bowl, whisk the cornmeal, buttermilk, egg, and browned butter until a thick, grainy batter forms. Carefully pour the batter into the skillet and spread it in an even layer all the way to the edges. Do not mix it into the potpie filling.

6 Line a baking sheet with parchment paper and place the skillet on top. Bake until the top browns, about 20 minutes.

TIP: How to Brown Butter

I simply put the butter into a large microwave-safe measuring cup and cook on high for 1½ to 2½ minutes. It will boil, then foam up, which is why you want a large measuring cup, and then it will come back down. This is when the milk solids begin to brown. Keep an eye on it at 1½ minutes and remove it if it browns quickly. If you are browning up to a whole stick, it usually takes about 3 minutes, depending on the wattage of your microwave.

THIS TRADITION SERVED THEM WELL

Mary from next door always fixed a pot of kraut and sausage. When she first married her husband Charlie, they boarded with a woman who brought this to them that first New Year's Day and told them that it would bring them luck, fortune, and good health. They ate it sitting on apple crates at a makeshift table because they hadn't had the money to buy a proper table and chairs. That year, they did so well that on New Year's Day Mary fixed a pot and they ate it at the table they'd bought. She said they had it every year since, and that every year they had what they needed, so it served them well. She always made sure I had a plate of it too, and every so many years, I make a pot myself.

RB's Fish Fry and Hushpuppies

My father-in-law fished his whole life. It was practically all he did in his spare time—and he made sure he had lots of spare time, even though Mick's mom tried to find other things that needed done. I told him that I wanted to go out on the boat with him some Saturday and fish. I hadn't fished since I was a kid, and that was from the bank of a pond a couple of times; my neighbor Charlie took me once to the river, and we tried to fish from the bridge, but it just wasn't a good day.

So, RB (yes, his name was RB) took me out, and I had such a good time that he bought me a pole for my birthday. I'd meet him before sunup at his campsite, and we'd put the boat in as the sun came up. He'd bring some breakfast onto the boat and I'd bring some coffee. He taught me to tie a line, to cast, and to reel it in. We'd toss whatever we'd caught into the holding tank and then clean them once we got back. I miss those Saturdays on the lake. He wanted us to take the boat out when he no longer could, but I just didn't know the lake like he did, and I couldn't back the boat into the water if my life depended on it. That's one thing he never could teach me, and he had the broken ribs to prove it because I almost ran him over, knocking him off the boat ramp.

A fish fry was his second favorite thing. He'd fry up a mess and make a pile of hushpuppies. When he got sick, I told him I wanted to know what he did, so he told me. I like to bread the fish and let it rest while I make the batter for the hushpuppies. Then while I fry the fish, the batter is resting. When the fish is done, I add a little more oil to the skillet and let it get hot and then fry up the hushpuppies. It's simple, just as a life spent fishing on the lake should be. And when it comes to the cornmeal, I always use a stone-ground, plain unbolted (which means unsifted) cornmeal. You can use white or yellow, but I prefer yellow.

YIELD 4 servings | **SEASONS ENJOYED** Summer

Fish Fry

1½ to 2 pounds (680 to 907 g) catfish fillets
½ to ¾ cup (120 to 180 ml) milk
1 cup (155 g) white or yellow plain cornmeal
⅓ cup (40 g) self-rising flour
½ teaspoon salt
¼ teaspoon black pepper
3 to 4 cups (720 to 960 ml) vegetable oil

Hushpuppies

⅔ cup (103 g) cornmeal
⅓ cup (40 g) self-rising flour
½ teaspoon salt
¼ teaspoon black pepper
1 teaspoon sugar
1 large egg
½ cup (120 ml) milk
2 to 3 tablespoons finely chopped onion
1 to 2 tablespoons finely chopped green bell pepper (optional)

continued on following page

continued from previous page

I RECKON YOU COULD
RB said if he had the green bell pepper, he liked to dice it and add it into the hushpuppy batter because it "added good flavor." This fry is great served with my Coleslaw (page 110) and some Deviled Eggs (page 106). He rarely drank, but a cold beer on a hot summer afternoon goes pretty well too.

1 To make the fish fry: Trim the fillets and check for any remaining bones. In a large bowl, add the fillets and pour the milk over, making sure they are completely covered. Let them rest while you prepare the cornmeal dredge.

2 In a shallow dish, stir together the cornmeal, flour, salt, and pepper. Working one at a time, dredge the fillets in the breading on both sides and lay them on a baking sheet to set. Make more breading if needed to finish them all. Let them rest a couple of minutes to set the breading.

3 Prep the hushpuppies: In a large bowl, stir together the cornmeal, flour, salt, pepper, sugar, egg, milk, onions, and if using, the green pepper until a thick batter forms. You want it to be just thick enough to hold onto a spoon and easy to push off with a finger. Add more flour if it's too thin or more milk if too thick.

4 In a large, deep cast-iron skillet over medium heat, heat about ½ inch (12 mm) of oil until it shimmers, about 2 minutes. Add as many fish fillets as will fit in the pan and fry until golden brown all over, 3 to 5 minutes per side. Transfer to a platter and repeat with the remaining fillets.

5 Add more oil to the skillet, enough to fill it with about 1½ inches (4 cm) of oil, and let it get hot (it will shimmer when it's ready).

6 Working in batches to avoid overcrowding the pan, scoop a tablespoon of batter and slide it off into the hot oil. Fry, making sure to turn them, until golden brown on all sides, 3 to 4 minutes. Using a slotted spoon, transfer the hushpuppies to a paper towel-lined platter to drain. Serve warm with the fish.

RB, my father-in-law. I miss those Saturday mornings out on the lake.

Salads & Sides

Deviled Eggs

We live by what my grandmaw said every time we walked in the door: "Have you eat yet?" When it starts to feel like summer, you'll find us having one of our screen-porch suppers. There's always plenty of food and more conversation than you can handle. And it doesn't matter if you've already eaten, there's still something worth pickin' at.

At our house, a screen-porch supper is almost never complete without some deviled eggs, which I've taken to calling the Devil's Cackleberries. They're one of the first things I remember learning how to make without a recipe. I watched Mom make 'em many times; she used dry mustard, but I just use good ole yellow mustard. The Devil's Cackleberries are something that you really make by taste, so adjustments are to be expected.

Let's talk about how to get the best results:

- Eggs that are a couple of weeks old peel better when hard-boiled..
- Turn the eggs over in the carton the night before you boil them so the yolks settle to the center
- Always boil one or two more than you plan to devil. That way if you get the yolk mixture too runny, you can mash in more yolk, and it will thicken right up. Then you'll have a couple of testers to make sure they're just right.
- Hide a batch of your own in the fridge to have once everyone leaves because they will eat them all.

YIELD 2 dozen deviled eggs | **SEASONS ENJOYED** Can I eat them seven days a week?

12 large eggs

2 to 3 tablespoons mayonnaise

1 to 2 tablespoons yellow mustard, divided

1 to 2 tablespoons Bread-and-Butter Pickle brine (page 26), divided

1 to 2 teaspoons white vinegar, divided

Salt and black pepper

Smoked paprika, for garnish

1 Place the eggs in a large pot and cover with at least 1 inch (2.5 cm)of water. Heat to boiling over high heat, then reduce the heat to medium-high and cook for 12 to 15 minutes.

2 Remove from the heat. Immediately and carefully drain the water and refill the pot with cold water. When the water turns warm, drain and refill with cold water again. Repeat this until the eggs are cool to the touch, about three times. Drain and refill one more time with cold water and put the lid back on. Over the sink, give the pot a good shake for about 30 seconds to crack the shells and help to start peeling them. Drain the water, peel the eggs, and halve them lengthwise.

3 Remove the yolks and put them in a small bowl. Using a fork, mash the yolks. Add to that the mayonnaise, 1 tablespoon of the mustard, 1 tablespoon of the pickle brine, 1 teaspoon of the vinegar, and the salt and pepper to taste. Mix until smooth and creamy. Taste to see what you might need more of and add any of the remaining mustard, pickle brine, and/or vinegar. You can always add more, but you can't take it out.

4 Using a spoon, fill each egg half with some of the yolk mixture. Sprinkle with a little paprika and serve.

I RECKON YOU COULD

If you're feeling fancy, you can pipe the yolks in and garnish with other things like crumbled bacon, a little relish, chives, or diced pimentos.

Golden Potato Salad

I think this potato salad is best made with my homemade Bread-and-Butter Pickles (page 26), but if you don't have time to make those, store-bought should work. I prefer gold potatoes and, since they have such thin skin, sometimes I leave the skins on, but that's entirely up to you. This recipe makes enough for a crowd, but if it's just you, there's nothing wrong with having a few days' worth of leftovers in the fridge. This is also a recipe that you have to taste and adjust for what you like. You can serve it immediately, but it's best after it sits in the fridge for a couple of hours to overnight so that the flavors come together and the salad is nice and cold.

YIELD 8 to 10 servings | **SEASONS ENJOYED** Spring, summer

2½ to 3 pounds (1.1 to 1.4 kg) gold potatoes, peeled and cut into equal-size chunks

4 hard-boiled eggs, diced

¼ cup (40 g) diced onion

¼ cup (36 g) diced Bread-and-Butter Pickles (page 26), plus 1 to 2 tablespoons brine

½ cup (120 ml) mayonnaise

¼ cup (60 ml) yellow mustard

2 tablespoons white vinegar

1 tablespoon sugar

1 teaspoon salt

1 teaspoon black pepper

1 Add the potatoes to a large pot and cover with water. Heat to boiling over high heat. Reduce the heat to medium-low, cover, and simmer until the potatoes are fork-tender, 10 to 12 minutes.

2 Drain the potatoes and immediately pour cold water over them to stop them from cooking any further. Drain and repeat a few times until the potatoes are cold, then transfer to a large bowl.

3 Add the hard-boiled eggs, onions, pickles, mayonnaise, mustard, vinegar, sugar, salt, and pepper. Gently fold the ingredients together. The potatoes will soften on the edges, which will help thicken the salad and bind everything together. Taste to see if it needs anything; depending on your preference for tangy or sweet, you may need more vinegar, pickle brine, or sugar. Add just a teaspoon at a time and stir well to combine before tasting again and adjusting. Refrigerate for 1 to 2 hours or overnight. Serve cold.

Coleslaw

This recipe is so easy to remember and is one that can be passed on by word of mouth. It's a riddle, sort of. To make it, just remember "a whole, half, half, quarter, quarter, dash, dash!" I don't know if anyone shared this with me, or if I just came up with it making it one day. I must insist on using fresh cabbage and shredding it yourself. Pre-shredded and bagged cabbage is okay, but fresh cabbage will wilt better. As it sits, it releases some of its water, adding even more flavor to the dressing. The dressing is also pretty flexible and can dress as little has half a cabbage or as much as two cabbages, depending on how creamy you prefer your slaw. I like to make this several hours to a day ahead to give the flavors time to come together. When I shred mine, I use a box grater, or as Mary from next door called it, the old knuckle buster. I like a coarse shred on this, but if you prefer long strips of cabbage, by all means cut it with a knife.

YIELD 15 to 20 servings | **SEASONS ENJOYED** Spring, summer

I RECKON YOU COULD
If you'd like to add some color, you can use purple cabbage in it, shred in a little carrot, or even a little bell pepper. Just know all those things will change the flavor just a bit, so do it to your liking.

1 whole head green cabbage, quartered and cored
½ cup (120 ml) mayonnaise
½ cup (100 g) sugar
¼ cup (60 ml) buttermilk
¼ cup (60 ml) white vinegar
Salt and black pepper

1 In a large bowl, using a box grater, shred the cabbage. Add the mayonnaise, sugar, buttermilk, and vinegar. Stir to combine. Add salt and pepper to taste.

2 Let sit for 1 to 2 hours or overnight. As it sits, the dressing can settle to the bottom, so give it a little stir occasionally. Stir well before serving to coat everything evenly. Adjust any ingredients to taste. Serve cold.

Marinated Bean Salad

My aunt Alice has been making this for decades, and it's one of the most delicious bean salads I have ever had. I've been known to sneak into the kitchen late in the evening just to get a few more spoonfuls before bed! Because of the vinegar-based dressing, it keeps very well for several days. And since it is not a mayonnaise- or dairy-based dressing, it can withstand being out of the refrigerator for a few hours, making it safe to travel. But it's best when served cold.

YIELD 12 to 14 servings | **SEASON ENJOYED** Summer

2 cans (14.5 ounces/411 g each) cut green beans

1 can (14.5 ounces/411 g) cut wax beans

1 can (15.8 ounces/448 g) great northern beans

1 can (15.5 ounces/439 g) dark red kidney beans

1 cup (160 g) diced yellow onion

½ cup (50 g) chopped scallions or spring onions, with some green

1 cup (100 g) chopped celery

1½ to 2 cups (180 to 240 g) diced bell pepper (color of choice)

1 teaspoon salt

½ cup (120 ml) white vinegar

½ cup (120 ml) canola or vegetable oil

½ cup (100 g) sugar

1 Drain and rinse all the beans and add them to a 4-quart (4 L) or larger nonaluminum pot.

2 Add the onions, scallions, celery, bell peppers, salt, vinegar, oil, and sugar. Stir well to combine and cook over medium heat until completely warmed through and the sugar dissolves, 5 to 7 minutes.

3 Remove from the heat and let it cool for about 20 minutes. Transfer it to a large serving bowl with a lid and refrigerate overnight. Serve cold.

Mick's Baked Beans

When I was growing up, Mom always made baked beans for picnics. Hers was just cooked on the stove and then she poured it into a baking dish and baked it just long enough to brown the beans on top a little. I always loved them, but when Mick made his baked beans to take to his parents that first Christmas dinner with them, I was hooked. This is one recipe that so many people have asked for over the years, too. It's a bit involved, but so worth the extra steps. When I pulled out his recipe, I could see all the stains on it from where it was within splattering-shot of the pan as he mixed it up over the years. That's also how you know it's a family favorite. There's nothing more validating than a well-worn and stained recipe card.

YIELD 8 to 10 servings | **SEASONS ENJOYED** Summer and holidays

1 pound (454 g) bacon
2 pounds (907 g) ground beef
2 cans (15 ounces/425 g each) pork and beans
1 tablespoon minced garlic
1 package (2 ounces) dry onion soup mix
½ cup (120 ml) ketchup
½ cup (110 g) packed brown sugar
1 tablespoon yellow mustard
1 tablespoon white vinegar

1 Preheat the oven to 350°F (175°C/gas 4).

2 In a large skillet over medium heat, cook the bacon until crispy. Transfer to a paper towel-lined plate, then crumble the bacon after it has slightly cooled.

3 Drain the fat from the skillet, then add the ground beef and cook, breaking it up with a wooden spoon, until browned, 8 to 10 minutes. Drain the fat.

4 In a 9 x 13-inch (23 by 33 cm) baking dish, add the pork and beans, garlic, onion soup mix, ketchup, brown sugar, mustard, vinegar, ½ cup (120 ml) of water, the cooked ground beef, and half the crumbled bacon; stir to combine well, then top with the remaining crumbled bacon.

5 Cover with foil and bake for 30 minutes. Remove the foil and bake until the top begins to brown, 10 to 15 minutes.

Appalachian Skillet Cornbread Dressing

I make cornbread dressing every time I cook a turkey, even though I'm the only one who will eat dressing of any kind. Well, my father-in-law did. He and I liked many of the same things. My Grandmaw Barton always had dressing on the table at any holiday meal. Hers was made with white bread, rings of onions, and lots of parsley. I loved it, but I really liked the cornbread dressing they would make in the school cafeteria. I know, but let me tell you, we had some good cooks in our schools. I have community cookbooks with many recipes from those ladies. It was scooped out into large balls and baked so it was crispy all over, then we would get a ladle of gravy over it and some sliced turkey. It was really good. For this, I kind of split the difference between the two. It's a little wet to start, so I don't think I could scoop it into balls, and I make mine in a cast-iron skillet to get those crispy edges.

YIELD 6 to 8 servings | **SEASONS ENJOYED** Fall, winter

I RECKON YOU COULD
Follow the directions for Pot Roast Gravy (page 50), using the drippings and broth from your Roast Turkey (page 84).

- 2 tablespoons bacon grease or turkey grease from the drippings
- ½ medium onion, diced
- 1 teaspoon minced garlic
- 4 to 5 slices white bread, cubed and toasted
- ½ pan Brown Butter Cornbread (page 60), crumbled
- ½ sleeve (16 to 18) saltine crackers, crushed (or butter crackers if you're feelin' fancy)
- 1 tablespoon chopped fresh sage or 1 teaspoon dried sage
- 1 teaspoon chopped fresh rosemary or ½ teaspoon dried rosemary
- 1 teaspoon fresh thyme or ½ teaspoon dried thyme
- 2 tablespoons chopped fresh parsley or 1 tablespoon dried
- ½ teaspoon salt
- 1 teaspoon black pepper
- 2 to 3 cups (480 to 720 ml) turkey broth, enough to make it wet, but not soupy
- Gravy of choice, for serving

1 Preheat the oven to 350°F (175°C/gas 4).

2 In a 10- to 12-inch (25 to 30 cm) skillet over medium heat, heat the grease until shimmering, about 2 minutes. Add the onions and cook, stirring occasionally, until translucent, 4 to 5 minutes. In the last minute, stir in the garlic.

3 In a large bowl, add the white bread, cornbread, crackers, sage, rosemary, thyme, parsley, salt, pepper, broth, and the sauteed onions and garlic; stir to combine. Transfer it all to the skillet. Cover with foil and bake for 30 minutes.

4 Remove the foil and bake until golden and crispy on top, 5 to 10 minutes. Serve warm with gravy.

Grandmaw's Baked Squash

I'm not one to use canned soups in a recipe, but I found this in Grandmaw's recipe box. I tried it for a family meal, and there was nothing left of it. So, it's a keeper.

YIELD 4 to 6 servings | **SEASONS ENJOYED** Summer, fall

4 tablespoons salted butter, melted, divided
¼ cup (60 ml) mayonnaise
1 tablespoon minced onion or scallion
2 large eggs
1 can (10.5 ounces/298 g) cream of chicken soup
½ cup (120 ml) milk
2 to 3 medium straight or crookneck yellow squash, cut into ½-inch (12 mm) cubes
1 sleeve butter crackers, crushed

1 Preheat the oven to 350°F (175°C/gas 4).

2 In a large bowl, stir together 1 tablespoon of the melted butter, the mayonnaise, onions, eggs, soup, and milk.

3 In a small bowl, stir together the remaining 3 tablespoons of the melted butter and the crackers.

4 In a 10-inch (25 cm) cast-iron skillet. Add the squash and pour the soup mixture over it, then sprinkle the buttery crackers over the top. Cover with foil and bake until the squash is fork-tender, 40 to 45 minutes. Remove the foil and bake until browned on top, 5 to 10 minutes. Serve warm.

Pure Appalachian Umami

Leather Britches are green beans that have been dried to preserve them. It's probably one of the most iconic Appalachian dishes you'll find. Before canning or freezing, drying was the most effective way to preserve foods. Done correctly, it can preserve things like beans for more than a year or two. Some foods, like herbs, can begin to lose their flavor after too long when dried, but these beans become more concentrated in flavor.

I can still remember the first time I knew what Leather Britches, also called Shuck Beans, Shucky Beans, or Shucks, were. In our house, we just referred to all green beans as string beans. Not all beans have strings, but for those that do, if you don't pull that string off (which we just call stringing), and you cook 'em, you won't be able to eat 'em. The string is tough and, to me, is as bad as getting shell in your scrambled eggs or bones in your fish. I can't stand it and can't eat 'em. To string your beans, pull back on the stem end to snap it and pull down the back side of the bean pod, and the string will pull off along with it. Then do the same with the bottom tip of the pod and pull the string off the front. Toss the ends and strings in your compost bin.

I was probably about nine or ten, and we were visiting another church in our area for something, probably a homecoming, and there was a dinner after the service. Some of the women of the church were in the kitchen in the social hall downstairs getting things ready. When we got there, Mom sent me down with our dish. I don't remember what we took, but it was probably a marble cake. That was her go-to for a potluck where she wanted to take something a little fancier. Anyway, I took it down, they wrote our last name on a piece of masking tape and stuck it on the bottom. I don't know if Mom just forgot or if she sent me down with it so they didn't give her a look for showing up without her dish marked.

I could smell everything else that had been brought. There was ham heating up in the oven, and meatloaf, and certainly fried chicken. I could see all kinds of sides like mashed potatoes, potato salad, and deviled eggs. I have such a weakness for deviled eggs. They were cutting up cakes and pies and putting them on plates to set out on the dessert table. No one ever took more than one dessert at a time, but if they did, they made sure to tell everyone who saw them that they were getting one for someone else. I'm not saying they lied, because it was church, but I'm sure my dad would have said that as he grabbed an extra piece of his favorite pineapple upside-down cake, which Mom might turn down and he'd then have to eat. After that first round, seconds were always welcome.

After service, we all headed downstairs and, as guests, we got to go first. I remembered a white-haired woman telling me, "Those are Leather Britches," pointing at the dish of green beans, and another woman said, "We call 'em Shucky Beans." I dipped some up and filled my plate. I found a seat and sat down at the table. I remember it had a Formica top with little square flecks in it and a chrome band all around the edge. The edge of it had chrome-headed nails every so many inches and I would run my fingers along the edge to feel them. I don't know why details like that stick in my mind all these years later, but they do.

When I took my first bite of the beans, I remembered tasting them before. They had a strong flavor that I called earthy, because it reminded me of what the garden dirt smelled like. Earthy flavors in vegetables are my favorite. Today we call that umami—more specifically Appalachian umami. They were seasoned with country ham, making 'em a little salty. The outer part of the bean almost melted in my mouth and the beans inside almost tasted like meat.

It was a while before I knew how they were dried, instead of canned, to preserve them. I've been drying Leather Britches now for a few years and save a string or two for Christmas dinner. I started growing greasy beans just so I could dry 'em. You can also use half-runners or any bean that has a smooth pod. Fuzzy beans aren't good for this. You start by rinsing them in cold water to get dirt off, and then let 'em dry before stringing 'em up. Prep a needle and thread. I use fishing line just because I have that and often can't find the thread. Then remember to string your string beans before you string your string beans!

You can leave the bean whole from there or go ahead and break it into smaller pieces. I like to leave them whole. Take a piece of line about two feet long and thread it through a needle just enough to hold the thread. I tie an old button on the end to keep the bean from breaking off, but some folks will wrap the first bean with several rounds of thread before moving on to the rest. Then take the needle and pass it through the middle of the bean, sliding the bean down to the end of the thread. Repeat with the rest of your beans until you have about 12 to 18 inches (30.5 to 46 cm) of beans, which for me is usually three-quarters to a whole pound per string.

Once you've got your string of beans, tie a loop at the top and hang the beans in a dry place with good ventilation, out of the sun. Where I live in East Tennessee, it gets pretty humid outside, so I hang mine in the back room of the house. I just have some nails at the top of the wall so they hang high. I'll leave 'em there for a couple of months until they're completely dry. I check on 'em every few days for the first two to three weeks to make sure I don't see any mold or bugs. If any beans go bad, just break them off the string. Once they're completely dried, you can pull them down and store in a paper bag. You don't want to use a plastic bag just in case they still have some moisture to them. To keep away bugs, toss a teaspoon of salt in the bag and tie it shut. Store the bag in the pantry where it can stay dry.

Before cooking your Leather Britches put them in a large bowl or pot with lots of water. They will float at this point, so you need lots of water to be able to move them around without breaking them apart. Gently stir them and let the water go still so any dust and dirt can float to the top. Pour off that water and repeat one to two more times. Then fill it once more and let them sit for a few hours to overnight, covered. After soaking they should be somewhat soft.

Leather Britches

When you're ready to cook 'em, this is my favorite way. I like to use biscuit-cut slices of country ham or cubed bacon to season them. I don't salt mine until the end because, depending on how salty my ham or bacon is, it may not need it. I taste the broth, which we call pot likker, at the end to see if it needs it. I love to dip warm cornbread in the pot likker, letting it soak up all that flavor. As they cook, don't let them dry out. You'll probably need to add a little hot water occasionally until they're done.

YIELD 4 to 6 servings | **SEASONS ENJOYED** Fall, winter

1 tablespoon lard, bacon grease, or vegetable oil

1 large onion, diced

3 to 4 biscuit-cut slices of country ham

1 tablespoon minced garlic

2 strings dried green beans (112 g), soaked a few hours to overnight and drained

Salt and black pepper

I RECKON YOU COULD

You can replace up to half of the water with pork, chicken, or beef broth.

1 In a large pot over medium heat, heat the fat until it shimmers, about 2 minutes. Add the onions and cook, stirring occasionally, until tender, about 10 minutes. In the last minute, add the ham and garlic; stir constantly until the garlic is lightly toasted.

2 Add the beans and enough water to cover everything by 2 inches (5 cm). Heat to boiling over high heat, then reduce the heat to low, cover, and simmer, stirring occasionally and adding water as needed, until the skins are translucent and the beans are tender and creamy and melt in your mouth, 3 to 4 hours. As they near being done, they don't need to be swimming, but you want to be able to see the broth just below the top of the beans. Taste the broth and season with salt and pepper to taste. Serve them warm as a side dish or as your main along with some cornbread.

Party Foods & Beverages

Grandaddy and Grandmaw Edge, 1961

Mountaineers Are Always Free! Especially on West Virginia Day.

The first time I remember Grandmaw Edge making pepperoni rolls was for my birthday. I had spent a couple of weeks with my great-grandparents in their house in Buckhannon, West Virginia. It was a huge two-story house with a big front porch. I know this was the summer between ninth and tenth grade, because I had taken art in high school my freshman year and really got into drawing. I took my sketchpad with me and sat on the wall in front of the Bicentennial Motel on Main Street, which was just across the street, and drew their house. I gave the drawing to Granddaddy for Father's Day, and today my aunt has it in the dining room of her house. The rest of my family came that week to spend a couple of days before we all went home.

Because I thought the world revolved around my then-teenage self, what I didn't realize was that those were West Virginia pepperoni rolls, and we really had them at dinner because it was West Virginia Day. Yep, I was born on West Virginia Day, which is June 20, the day it became a state in 1863. How's that for being a true Appalachian! If you're from West Virginia, you know what a pepperoni roll is. If you're not, it's just what it sounds like: a roll with pepperoni baked inside. These came about because a wife baked them for her husband who worked in the coal mines. A miner's pail could easily hold four to six of them, and there was no worry about spoilage. It became a huge thing, and all the miners ate them. You can find them almost anywhere across the state today. Grandmaw was born and raised in Webster, West Virginia and had plenty of family that worked in the coal mines.

My great-granddaddy was a baker in Buckhannon. He really wanted to be a baseball player, and even made the minor leagues, but Great-Grandmaw wouldn't hear of it, so he got a regular job. I'm sure he made thousands of pepperoni rolls in his lifetime. I remember him, but just barely. I thought he looked just like George Burns, right down to the cigar, which he would tamp out and stick in his shirt pocket. He was always wearing a dress shirt, many of them with a little brown or burnt spot in the pocket, usually because a cigar burned through his pocket protector.

I helped Grandmaw stuff the rolls on my birthday to get ready to bake. She had me lay three slices of pepperoni on each, then she rolled them up. They were small and appetizer sized. She asked me what cake I wanted for my birthday. I didn't really know what to say—I hadn't been asked that before. As I was the fourth kid, we didn't really celebrate my birthday much; I think my parents were just tired by the time I came along. I asked for pineapple upside-down cake. Maybe that's why I feel like it's kind of a fancy and impressive cake.

Grandmaw's Pepperoni Rolls

You'll see lots of recipes made with pizza sauce, cheese, herbs, and all kinds of things in them, but these are a classic pepperoni roll, made with Grandmaw's Refrigerator Rolls (page 56).

YIELD 1 dozen rolls | **SEASONS ENJOYED** Summer

12 golf ball–size dough balls from Grandmaw's Refrigerator Rolls (page 56)

36 pepperoni slices

1 tablespoon salted butter, melted

1 Flatten a dough ball out in your fingers, stretching it out to a 3-inch (7.5 cm) round.

2 Lay 2 pepperoni slices on the edge of the flat round and pull the dough halfway over the slices as you begin to roll it up. Then lay another slice right in the middle and continue rolling to completely cover all 3 slices. Tuck the ends under and place on a baking sheet. Repeat with the remaining dough and pepperoni.

3 Preheat the oven to 400°F (205°C/gas 6). Cover the rolls with a clean kitchen towel let them rise while the oven comes to temperature, 15 to 20 minutes.

4 Brush the rolls with the melted butter and bake until golden brown on top, 15 to 18 minutes. Transfer the rolls to a serving platter and serve warm. If you prefer, serve with marinara sauce or ranch dressing for dipping.

Sausage Balls

A lot of people make these with a biscuit mix, but they're just as easy to make from scratch. And, you know what's in them. When it comes to the cheese, I like to shred my own. The packaged shredded cheddar has a coating on it that makes it harder for the shreds to stick together, and the cheese doesn't melt as well. If you have access to ground sausage from a local farmer or butcher, it can make all the difference in how these taste. It might cost a little more, but you help support a local maker. To quickly soften the cream cheese, fill a bowl big enough to hold the wrapped block of cream cheese with very warm water and let the unwrapped block sit in it for 15 minutes.

YIELD 4 dozen | **SEASONS ENJOYED** Spring, summer, fall, winter

1¼ cups (150 g) plain flour
2 teaspoons baking powder
½ teaspoon salt
1 teaspoon sugar
¼ cup (50 g) shortening
1 block (8 ounces/227 g) cream cheese, softened
2 cups (227 g) shredded cheddar cheese
1 pound (454 g) mild or hot sausage

I RECKON YOU COULD
For a little something extra, use a pepper-jack cheese. Or try a cranberry cheese for a festive holiday flavor. If you can't find that, chop up ¼ cup (37 g) of dried cranberries and add them into the mix.

1 Preheat the oven to 400°F (205°C/gas 6). Line a rimmed baking sheet with parchment paper.

2 In a large bowl, sift together the flour, baking powder, salt, and sugar. Using a pastry blender, cut in the shortening until the mixture resembles coarse meal. Add the cream cheese, cheddar cheese, and raw sausage and mix with your hands until you no longer see any bits of dry mix.

3 Using a small cookie scoop or a rounded tablespoon measure, scoop the mixture and roll it into 1- to 1½-inch (2.5 to 4 cm) balls and place them on the prepared baking sheet, 1 inch (2.5 cm) apart.

4 Bake until browned, 25 to 30 minutes, rotating the pan halfway through. Transfer to a paper towel–lined plate to drain for a minute. Serve warm.

Bacon Spinach Artichoke Dip

What's a party without a dip? This is a slight twist on the traditional spinach artichoke dip, with the addition of bacon; it's extra cheesy, with three different types of cheese. Perfect for game day. We love to serve this with crackers, pita chips, tortilla chips, toasted bread slices, or make the Biscuit Dough Crackers (page 136).

YIELD 6 to 8 servings | **SEASONS ENJOYED** Fall, winter

2 jars (12 ounces/340 g each) artichoke hearts in water, drained

2 bags (10 ounces/283 g each) frozen chopped spinach, thawed and squeezed dry

6 strips chopped crispy bacon, divided

1 block (8 ounces/227 g) cream cheese, softened

¾ cup (180 ml) sour cream

¾ cup (180 ml) mayonnaise

2 teaspoons minced garlic

1½ cups (150 g) shredded Parmesan cheese, divided

¾ cup (85 g) shredded mozzarella cheese, divided

¾ cup (85 g) shredded cheddar cheese, divided

1 Preheat the oven to 350°F (175°C/gas 4).

2 In a large bowl, add the artichoke hearts, spinach, 4 strips of the chopped bacon, cream cheese, sour cream, mayonnaise, garlic, 1 cup (100 g) of the Parmesan cheese, ½ cup (55 g) of the mozzarella, and ½ cup (55 g) of the cheddar cheese; stir to combine.

3 Spread the mixture into a 12-inch (30 cm) cast-iron skillet and top with the remaining ½ cup (50 g) Parmesan, the remaining ¼ cup (30 g) mozzarella, and the remaining ¼ cup (30 g) cheddar cheese, and the remaining chopped bacon.

4 Bake until the top is bubbly and beginning to brown, 20 to 25 minutes. Serve warm.

LODGE

Cilantro Lime Chicken Wings

The zing of the lime juice and the light heat of the red pepper flakes make these wings crave-able. Now these may not seem very Appalachian, but they were one of the first things that Mick and I made up on our own, just in time for the Super Bowl. The flavor the lime juice gives them reminds me of the vinegary taste of the Shenandoah BBQ Chicken (page 92). We like the whole wings for these, but for a crowd, you can use the mini drums and flaps, so you have plenty to go 'round.

YIELD 4 to 6 servings | **SEASONS ENJOYED** Spring, summer, fall, winter

Grated zest of 1 lime

½ cup (120 ml) fresh lime juice (about 4 limes)

1 teaspoon salt

½ teaspoon pepper

½ teaspoon crushed red pepper flakes

1 bunch cilantro, leaves and tender stems chopped (about ⅓ cup/20 g)

¾ cup (180 ml) extra-virgin olive oil

2 to 3 (0.9 to 1.4 kg) pounds chicken wings

1 In a large bowl, stir together the lime zest, juice, salt, pepper, red pepper flakes, cilantro, and olive oil. Reserve ⅓ cup (80 ml) of the marinade in the refrigerator. Place the wings in a large zip-top bag; add the remaining marinade, seal, and shake to make sure the pieces are evenly coated. Refrigerate for 2 to 4 hours or overnight.

2 Preheat the oven to 375°F (190°C/gas 5). Line a baking sheet with parchment paper and set a wire cooling rack on top.

3 Place the wings on the wire rack and transfer the used marinade to a small saucepan. Heat to boiling over high heat. Boil for 1 minute to kill any bacteria.

4 Bake the wings until golden brown, 45 to 50 minutes, basting with the boiled marinade every 8 to 10 minutes for the first 30 minutes. Discard the used marinade.

5 In a large glass or microwave-safe bowl, microwave the reserved marinade for 2 minutes. Add the wings and toss to coat. Serve warm and enjoy.

Biscuit Dough Crackers

When you're making my Flaky Layers Buttermilk Biscuits (page 38), you can save the unbaked scraps in an airtight container and freeze them for up to a month. When you have about 1½ cups (340 g) of scraps, you're ready to make the crackers. Serve these with your favorite spread, cheeseball, or my Bacon, Spinach, and Artichoke Dip (page 132).

YIELD 2 to 3 dozen | **SEASONS ENJOYED** Spring, summer, fall, winter

I RECKON YOU COULD
You could use an infused butter, like garlic or herb, to melt and brush on the crackers before baking. You could also sprinkle them with a little grated cheese of your choice before baking or just as soon as they come out of the oven.

Plain flour, for dusting
1½ cups (340 g) Flaky Layers Buttermilk Biscuits (page 38) dough scraps, thawed
Melted salted butter, for brushing
Kosher or flake salt, for sprinkling

1 Preheat oven to 375°F (190°C/gas 5). Line a baking sheet with parchment paper.

2 On a well-floured surface, use a well-floured rolling pin to roll out the dough to about ¼-inch (6 mm) thickness. Using a pizza cutter, cut the dough into 1- or 2-inch (2.5 or 5 cm) squares. Place the squares on the prepared baking sheet, about ½ inch (12 mm) apart. Prick each piece a couple of times with a fork. Brush them with the melted butter and sprinkle with a little salt.

3 Bake until golden brown and crispy, 10 to 12 minutes. Transfer to a cooling rack and let cool completely. Store in an airtight container for up to a week.

Sweet Iced Tea

Mary from next door always had some sweet tea in the refrigerator in the summer. She had a green glass pitcher that was all bubbly and bumpy, and a set of tall glasses to match. She'd get out a pot, put 2 cups (400 g) of sugar in it, and fill it up to within an inch (2.5 cm) of the top with water. Then she'd get 6 teabags out and tie the strings together and toss it in the pot. It would come to a boil and she'd let it simmer for just a minute, cut it off, and let it sit on the back burner to cool a bit.

Her ice trays were the old aluminum kind with the handle that you pulled back to break the cubes free. They matched the old Frigidaire they had with the big handle you had to pull like a slot machine to open. That green pitcher would get filled with ice. She'd pull the teabags out of the pot and give them a good squeeze, 'cause she wanted to get all the tea flavor out of 'em. The tea was poured into the pitcher, over the ice, and then she'd fill a glass with ice and fill those up. She'd offer a lemon slice if she had any lemons, but most of the time we just drank it straight.

I RECKON YOU COULD

In the fall and winter, you can add a ¼ teaspoon of ground cloves to the pot, along with the juice of 1 large orange, and bring it all to a boil. Serve as above over ice with an orange slice garnish for a Spiced Iced Tea.

Mary and me, Christmas 1994. This is the only picture I have of the two of us. I never saw her in the kitchen without her apron on.

Christmas Eve Eggnog

I love a good eggnog; it just tastes like Christmas. This one is creamy, thick, and very rich (as I think it should be). You can make it without the rum for a nonalcoholic version, but I think it adds to the nostalgic taste. Using fresh nutmeg really takes it to the next level in flavor.

YIELD 12 to 14 servings | **SEASONS ENJOYED** Winter

6 large eggs, whites and yolks separated, whites at room temperature

¾ cup (150 g) sugar, divided

2 cups (480 ml) heavy cream, divided

2 cups (480 ml) whole milk, divided

1 teaspoon ground cinnamon

¼ teaspoon freshly grated nutmeg, plus more for garnish

¼ cup (60 ml) spiced rum

1 teaspoon vanilla extract

1 In the bowl of a stand mixer fitted with the whisk attachment, beat the egg yolks and ½ cup (100 g) sugar at medium-high speed until light and smooth, about 2 minutes.

2 In a medium saucepan over medium-low heat, heat 1 cup (240 ml) of the cream, 1 cup (240 ml) of the milk, the cinnamon, and grated nutmeg to just hot, about 130°F (54°C). Slowly stream into the whipped egg yolks, while vigorously whisking, to temper the eggs, then pour it all back into the saucepan. Cook over medium-low heat, whisking continuously, until it thickens into a soft custard and reaches 180°F (82°C). Remove from the heat and stir in the remaining 1 cup (240 ml) cream, the remaining 1 cup (240 ml) milk, the rum, and vanilla. Let it cool for 30 minutes.

3 In the stand mixer, beat the egg whites at high speed until soft peaks form, about 2 minutes. Continuing at high speed, slowly add the remaining ¼ cup (50 g) sugar and beat until firm, but not stiff, peaks form, about 1 minute.

4 With a wire whisk, gently whisk the egg whites into the eggnog mixture. It will become very creamy. Chill for 3 to 4 hours, whisking each hour. Serve chilled with freshly grated nutmeg over each glass.

Punch for 50

Only a preacher's wife would have a recipe for punch to serve fifty people at a time! When going through Grandmaw's handwritten recipes, I found this on a piece of paper that was torn out of a notepad and folded so it would fit in the recipe box. It's worn around its edges and folds from all the times it must have been used. I would say this was served at many a "dinner on the ground" after church. These used to happen in the summers in Appalachia and the greater South. After service, everyone gathered outside the church, where tables might be set up under a large shade tree from a couple of boards over sawhorses with fresh white tablecloths thrown over them. Sometimes the tablecloths might just be laid out on the ground. The spreads would include lots of fried chicken, deviled eggs, and cakes of every kind. Folks brought blankets and tossed them out to sit on all around the church yard.

A dinner on the ground would be held as a fundraiser for the church for a building fund or mission work. Sometimes they would be called a homecoming, which I remember Granddaddy coming back to attend. Whatever the need, it was a time of community, and it brought out lots of people, so a punch like this was, and is, very refreshing. Mom made some version of this for Christmas Eve for several years.

YIELD 50 servings | **SEASONS ENJOYED** Spring, summer, fall, winter

3 cups (600 g) sugar

1 bottle (46 ounces/1.4 L) no-pulp orange juice, refrigerated

1 can (46 ounces/1.4 L) pineapple juice, refrigerated

1 quart (960 ml) ginger ale, refrigerated

1 pint (480 ml) any flavor sherbet

1 In a 3-quart (3 L) saucepan, add the sugar and 2½ cups (600 ml) of water; heat to boiling over high heat. Cook, stirring constantly, to make simple syrup, about 1 minute. Refrigerate overnight.

2 In a very large punch bowl or large pot, combine the orange juice, pineapple juice, ginger ale, and the chilled simple syrup with 5 cups (1.2 L) of water. Just before serving, scoop large scoops of the sherbet into the punch.

Triple-Chocolate Hot Cocoa Mix

Mom would sometimes make us a pot of hot chocolate on the stove on a cold snowy day. When my best friend's family moved into the neighborhood, us kids all ended up at their house during a heavy snowstorm. Her mom not only made us some hot chocolate on the stove, she made it a hot chocolate bar before those were even a thing. We had whipped cream and mini marshmallows to put on top, and she set out dishes of chocolate chips on the table. We spent the day going in and out to play in the snow. When we were in, we warmed up with mugs of hot chocolate, sitting by the fire, and stringing up popcorn so we could hang it from tree branches for the birds to eat.

I came up with this mix a few years ago, thinking about that day. The combination of regular and dark chocolate makes it so rich, and the white chocolate chips add that familiar vanilla taste like the real vanilla my friend's mom and my mom both stirred into the pot. I mix this up and store it in airtight containers so I can give some away as gifts, and the rest I drink all winter long. And yes, it goes great with a bowl of Snow Cream (page 179)!

I RECKON YOU COULD

Make about 37 mugs of cocoa from this mix.

For a kick, add a shot of bourbon, spiced rum, or Baileys Irish Cream. For spice, add a sprinkle of cinnamon, or a little sprinkle of cayenne pepper for some heat. For a butterscotch flavor, add a little maple syrup. I also like to drop a couple of tablespoons of the mix in my coffee in the mornings.

YIELD 7 cups (781 g) of mix | **SEASONS ENJOYED** Winter, especially in a snowstorm.

3 cups (84 g) nonfat powdered milk
2 cups (240 g) powdered sugar
1 cup (95 g) unsweetened milk chocolate cocoa powder
½ cup (50 g) unsweetened dark cocoa powder
1 bag (11 ounces/312 g) white chocolate chips
½ teaspoon salt

1 In a large bowl, stir together the powdered milk, powdered sugar, milk chocolate cocoa, dark cocoa, white chocolate chips, and salt.

2 In a food processor, process 2 to 3 cups (223 to 335 g) of the mix until the chocolate chips are fully ground and blended with the dry ingredients. Transfer to another large bowl and repeat with the remaining mix. Whisk all the batches together and store in airtight containers.

3 To make a cup of cocoa, add 3 tablespoons of mix to a large mug. Heat up 1 cup (240 ml) of water to boiling. Pour it into the mug and stir until the mix is completely dissolved. Top with some homemade marshmallows or whipped cream and enjoy.

Desserts & Sweets

World-Famous (in My World, so It's Famous Here) Carrot Cake

Several years ago, my Grandmaw Barton, Mom's mom, passed away at ninety-eight years old. That Christmas, I really wanted to make one of her cakes to remember her. Most of my Christmases growing up we would go to her house for dinner. Dinner for her started at 11 a.m. but was ready by 10 a.m. if you showed up early. Grandmaw would be up for hours making everything from scratch, but she baked for the whole week before.

She had a back room that she didn't heat in the winter and kept it closed off from the rest of the house. This was her cold room. She would tell Mom, "Now go in there and getcha' a cake and take home." Mom asked her a couple of times for the recipe. I think she worried that one day Grandmaw would be gone and she wouldn't have a slice of her cake ever again. Grandmaw would just say "Aw, I don't know. I just make it. It's got this 'n that in it." But Mom passed before Grandmaw did, so she never got the recipe. At Grandmaw's funeral, there were pictures of her life scrolling on TV screens at either end of the room on family night. A picture of my mom popped up that I hadn't seen before. She was sitting in the kitchen at Christmas in the chair by the window where Grandmaw sat and read each morning and night, mostly her Bible. Mom had a plate full of food in her lap, and there was a slice of cake to the side. There was also a picture on the wall of an old grist mill, five hundred miles (805 km) away, that I would end up working for a decade later. I'm still there today, but that's another story. I had no idea that picture was in her house. Now it's in my office.

I got to looking through all the cookbooks and clips that I had and I started playing around with some ingredients and baked the carrot cake. Then I thought I needed to make icing for it but wondered why Grandmaw never put icing on hers. That's when I realized I'd made the wrong cake. Mom always took home her applesauce cake, and what I'd made was carrot. This was Christmas Eve morning. I frantically began looking at more recipes, trying to figure out how to make an applesauce cake.

I made a list of ingredients and headed to the grocery store. I had enough time to bake an applesauce cake and make cream cheese icing for the carrot cake. I got to bed late and then up early, just like Grandmaw did. We were hosting all the family holiday meals at this point for my in-laws, so I had lots to get done. After dinner, I brought out the desserts. I told everyone what I'd done and had a good laugh about it. I cut myself a slice of the applesauce cake. I told them that I really wanted to have the first slice, even though I knew it would be rude to go ahead of my guests, but that it would mean a lot to me. I took a bite, then I looked up and said, "Grandmaw, this cake is exactly as I remember it. It's just as dry as yours was." I put my fork down, got another plate, and cut myself a slice of the carrot cake.

From that moment on, carrot cake was my cake, and I was resolved to Grandmaw having the applesauce cake as her legacy, dry as it was.

World-Famous Carrot Cake

My triple-layer carrot cake really has become kinda famous. I've made it for friends and fundraisers, and I knew that this was one recipe I would save for the cookbook.

YIELD 10 to 12 servings | **SEASONS ENJOYED** Spring, summer, fall, winter

Cake

2½ cups (300 g) plain flour

2½ teaspoons ground cinnamon

2½ teaspoons baking soda

¾ teaspoon salt

2½ cups (500 g) sugar

1 cup (240 ml) whole-fat buttermilk

4 large eggs

¾ cup (180 ml) vegetable oil

1 can (8 to 10 ounces/227 to 283 g) crushed pineapple, drained

½ cup (50 g) flaked or shredded coconut

1 cup (120 g) chopped pecans

2½ cups (275 g) freshly grated carrot

Cream Cheese Frosting

1 cup (2 sticks/227 g) salted butter, softened

2 blocks (8 ounces /227 g each) cream cheese, softened

5 cups (600 g) powdered sugar

1 tablespoon vanilla extract

1 Preheat the oven to 350°F (175°C/gas 4). Line three 8- to 9-inch (20 to 23 cm) cake pans with parchment paper rounds.

2 Make the cake: In a large bowl, sift together the flour, cinnamon, baking soda, and salt.

3 In the bowl of a stand mixer fitted with the paddle attachment, add the sugar and buttermilk. With the mixer at low speed, add 1 egg at a time, mixing until each egg is fully incorporated, then add the oil and mix to combine. With the mixer at low speed, add the flour mixture, 1 large spoonful at a time, mixing until no streaks of flour are visible, about 1 minute. Fold in the pineapple, coconut, pecans, and grated carrot.

4 Divide the batter equally among the cake pans. Bake on the middle rack until the sides begin to pull away from the pan and a cake tester inserted in the center comes out clean, 45 to 50 minutes.

5 Transfer the cakes to a wire rack and let cool for 10 to 15 minutes. Place the rack on top of a pan and invert; remove the pan, then the parchment paper. Repeat with the remaining cakes. Set the cakes on the rack, top side up, and let cool completely, 30 to 45 minutes.

6 Meanwhile, make the frosting: Using a stand mixer fitted with the paddle attachment, mix the butter and cream cheese at medium speed until smooth, about 2 to 3 minutes. Reduce the speed to low and add the powdered sugar, 1 cup at a time, until fully incorporated. Add the vanilla and mix until just incorporated, about 30 seconds. Do not overmix.

7 To assemble, place the first layer on a platter and top it with a layer of frosting, about ½ inch (12 mm) thick, spreading it to the edges evenly. Top it with the next layer, letting the frosting ooze out just a bit, and repeat. Once the third layer is on, spread the frosting on a little thicker. Decorate with additional pecan halves or pieces and some coconut.

I RECKON YOU COULD

If you plan on using a glass dome cake plate to display your cake, make sure it's an extra tall one! Sometimes I make a double layer for us and use the third layer cut in half for a double-layer half-cake that I can give away. This is something my grandmaw would have done if she'd made carrot cake.

Zucchini Bread

If you end up with a zucchini that's way too big to cook, shred it and make this bread. It makes enough to freeze or share. My best friend's mom, who was also a great friend of mine, gave me this recipe. It's dark and moist and so full of flavor. I've never had zucchini bread like it anywhere else.

YIELD 2 loaves | **SEASONS ENJOYED** Summer, fall

Cake Goop (page 21)
2 to 3 cups (300 to 450 g) peeled, seeded, and grated zucchini
3 large eggs
2 cups (400 g) sugar
¾ cup (180 ml) vegetable oil
2 tablespoons vanilla extract
2 cups (240 g) plain flour
2 tablespoons ground cinnamon
2 teaspoons baking soda
¼ teaspoon baking powder

I RECKON YOU COULD
Mom especially loved a slice of this warm in a bowl with some milk poured on top, and I have to say she was not wrong!

1 Preheat the oven to 350°F degrees (175°C/gas 4). Grease two 9-inch (23 cm) loaf pans with Cake Goop.

2 Put the grated zucchini in a colander and press out as much water as possible.

3 In a batter bowl, mix the eggs, sugar, oil, and vanilla and beat well.

4 In a large bowl, sift together the flour, cinnamon, baking soda, and baking powder.

5 Add the wet ingredients to the dry and, using a spatula, stir until a very thick batter forms. Fold in the grated zucchini and mix well. The batter will thin out quite a bit.

6 Divide the batter between the loaf pans and bake until the bread begins to pull away from the sides of the pans and a cake tester inserted in the center comes out clean, 50 to 60 minutes.

7 Transfer to a wire rack to cool for 30 minutes. Place the baking rack upside down on top of the pans and invert them. Pull the pans off and turn the loaves right-side up and let them finish cooling, about 30 minutes.

Pineapple Upside-Down Cake

If we were at a church dinner, you could count on Dad to put a piece or two of this at his place before he even got his plate together. It was always his favorite, and one of mine too. I met Mick a few months after my dad passed, and that first Father's Day without him was the first time I met Mick's dad. We went out to celebrate, and for dessert, he got a piece of pineapple upside-down cake. It also happened to be my birthday. All the signs were there (you know by now, I completely believe in signs) that this man would become my father-in-law for the rest of his life. I made it a mission to make the perfect pineapple upside-down cake. After some trial and error, my father-in-law gave it a thumbs up. I used to make him his own cake for holidays and his birthday. I've made it for small dinners about Appalachian cooking and cast-iron cooking, and one gentleman in his eighties was almost in tears as he told me that it was so close to his mother's that he couldn't believe it.

YIELD 8 servings | **SEASONS ENJOYED** Spring, summer, fall, winter

½ cup (1 stick/115 g) butter
1½ cups (180 g) plain flour
2 teaspoons baking powder
¼ teaspoon salt
⅓ cup (70 g) shortening
⅔ cup (135 g) granulated sugar
1 large egg
1 teaspoon vanilla extract
1 cup (240 ml) buttermilk
1 cup (220 g) packed light brown sugar
9 pineapple rings
9 maraschino cherries, plus more for garnish, if desired
Fresh whipped cream or ice cream, for serving, if desired

1 Preheat the oven to 350°F (175°C/gas 4). Place the butter in a 12-inch (30 cm) cast-iron skillet and set the skillet in the oven to heat up and melt the butter.

2 In a large bowl, sift together the flour, baking powder, and salt. In the bowl of a stand mixer fitted with the paddle attachment, beat the shortening and sugar at medium speed until light and fluffy, about 2 to 3 minutes. Add the egg and vanilla and mix at medium-low speed until incorporated. Add the buttermilk and mix until incorporated. Add the dry ingredients, one large spoonful at a time until no flour streaks are visible, at low speed. The batter will be thick and slightly firm.

3 When the butter has melted, remove the skillet from the oven and sprinkle the brown sugar evenly over the bottom. Lay the pineapple rings in a single layer and place a cherry in the center of each ring. If you like, place cherries in the corners between the rings. Spoon the batter over the pineapples and cherries and carefully spread it out to the edges of the skillet. Return the skillet to the oven and bake until the edges are golden brown and a cake tester inserted in the center comes out clean, 40 to 45 minutes.

4 Let the cake cool on a rack for 10 minutes. Place a platter over the skillet, invert, and leave it for a moment for the juices to drip down. If any pineapple rings or cherries stick to the skillet when you pull it off, just carefully remove them and place them on the cake—no one will ever know. (If they realize and point it out, then they don't get a second piece.) Serve it warm with some fresh whipped cream or ice cream if desired.

I RECKON YOU COULD

I made this a few times in my fluted cast-iron pan for my father-in-law, lining each curve with half pineapple rings with extra cherries in between. It was a bit of a showstopper. He loved it because it was loaded with twice the pineapple and cherries it would normally have.

Every now and then, I like to use some moonshine cherries just to give it a little extra kick, and it does!

Mock Apple Pie

When I put out my first garden after Charlie passed, it felt like I started learning all over again. I thought I'd paid attention, but things got out of control on me quickly. Zucchini is one of those things that can be a couple of inches long one day and a foot long the next. When they get too big, they're too seedy for cooking, but that makes them perfect for baking. The wife of my dad's best friend shared this recipe with me. I was so happy to find another way to use up the monstrous zukes that I had grown. I think I actually prefer this mock apple pie to a real one! When I make this, I prefer to use my All-Butter Pie Dough (page 71), because it feels more rustic to me.

YIELD 8 Servings | **SEASON ENJOYED** Summer

2 large zucchini
Juice of 1 lemon
2 tablespoons apple cider vinegar
1 cup (220 g) packed light brown sugar
¾ cup (150 g) granulated sugar
1½ teaspoons ground cinnamon
¼ teaspoon ground allspice
¼ teaspoon ground nutmeg
¼ teaspoon ground cardamom
⅛ teaspoon salt
2 tablespoons plain flour
2½ tablespoons cornstarch
1 recipe All-Butter Pie Dough (page 71)

1 Preheat the oven to 375°F (190°C/gas 5).

2 Peel the zucchini and halve it lengthwise. Scoop out the seeds and discard. Cut it crosswise into ¼-inch (6 mm) slices so they resemble apple slices.

3 In a large pot, heat 8 cups (2 L) of water to boiling over high heat. Add the zucchini slices and let the water return to a boil. Cook for 4 minutes then drain immediately; transfer to a large bowl, add the lemon juice, and vinegar and stir to coat evenly.

4 In a small bowl, stir together the brown sugar, white sugar, cinnamon, allspice, nutmeg, cardamom, salt, flour, and cornstarch. Sprinkle over the cooked zucchini and stir to coat.

5 Roll out the pie dough for the bottom crust to about 11½ inches (29 cm) and place it in a 9-inch (23 cm) pie pan. For the top, you can roll out the other dough to 9½ inches (24 cm) for a top crust, or use a crumble topping or crisp topping.

6 Add the filling to the pie dish. If using a top crust, lay it over the pie filling and trim it, along with the bottom crust, leaving about ½ inch (12 mm) overhang. Fold both layers under and crimp them together, pressing down on the rim of the pie plate to hold them in place. Cut 3 to 4 slits in the center for venting. Bake until the filling is noticeably bubbly, to ensure it sets fully, 40 to 45 minutes. Cover the crust with foil as needed to prevent burning. Let the pie cool completely before serving.

I RECKON YOU COULD

I made this for my best friend a few years ago. She was very skeptical, so I dressed it up by making the piecrust from layers of phyllo dough with butter brushed between them, and then a crumble top. It made a beautiful presentation and the crust was amazing. She not only loved it but asked for more! If you want to make a crisp topping, use the Christmas Crisp (page 166) and omit the mincemeat. Any unused crisp topping can be stored in an airtight container and frozen for up to 6 months.

Green Tomato Pie

In the late fall, just before the first frost threatens to bite, I pick the tomato vines clean. Any that are ripe or beginning to ripen will take their place on the windowsill in the kitchen. Any that are green get put to very good use. If they're big enough, I'll make us the last fried green tomatoes of the year. The small ones, about 2 to 2½ inches (5 to 6 cm) in diameter, are perfect for making this pie. You want them very green, because those have the fewest seeds and are mostly dry inside. This pie says goodbye to summer flavors and heralds fall with all the warm spices. The cumin can be a nice alternative to cinnamon, but I like them together. And, its slight citrusy flavor gives just a hint of summer, while the brown sugar lifts up the cinnamon, nutmeg, and cloves. I have a nutmeg grinder, which is just a little bowl with a Microplane on top, and I store whole nutmeg in it. When I need some ground, I just plane off what I need. I love the smell of it freshly ground. I like to use my Vodka Pie Dough (page 72) for this because it feels like a toast to send off summer!

YIELD 8 servings | **SEASON ENJOYED** Fall

- 3 tablespoons salted butter
- 2 pounds (907 g) small (2 to 2½ inches/5 to 6.3 cm diameter) green tomatoes, cored and cut into ½-inch-thick (12 mm) wedges
- 1¼ cups (275 g) packed brown sugar
- ¼ teaspoon ground nutmeg
- 1 teaspoon ground cinnamon
- ¼ teaspoon ground cloves
- ½ teaspoon ground cumin
- ½ teaspoon salt
- ¼ cup (30 g) plain flour
- 2 tablespoons apple cider vinegar
- 1 recipe Vodka Pie Dough (page 72)
- 1 large egg white, beaten with a splash of water
- 1 tablespoon coarse sugar
- Sprinkle of ground cinnamon

I RECKON YOU COULD
You can keep this pie at room temperature for 2 to 3 days or in the refrigerator for up to a week.

1 Preheat the oven to 375°F (190°C/gas 5).

2 In a large skillet over medium heat, melt the butter and add the tomato wedges, brown sugar, nutmeg, cinnamon, cloves, cumin, salt, flour, and vinegar. Toss everything around to coat the tomatoes well. Cook, stirring occasionally until thickened, about 5 minutes. It's thick enough when you can run a spoon through it and count to three before it comes back together. Remove from the heat.

3 Roll out the bottom layer of the piecrust about 1½ inches (4 cm) beyond the size of the pie dish and fit it in your pie pan or a 10-inch (25 cm) cast-iron skillet. Trim the edges to leave a 1-inch (2.5 cm) overhang. Add the tomato filling. Roll out the top layer of dough and place it in any pattern you prefer. You can make a lattice, solid top, or decorative top with cut dough. Fold the overhanging dough under, catching the top layer in it, and crimp the edges, locking the two crusts together. Brush the beaten egg white onto the crust. Sprinkle the coarse sugar all over, followed by a light sprinkling of cinnamon.

4 Line a baking sheet with parchment paper and place the pan on top. Bake until the filling is bubbly and the top is golden brown, about 1 hour. If needed, cover the crust with foil to prevent it from burning.

5 Let it cool completely on a cooling rack, about 1 hour. Serve with freshly whipped cream.

Appalachian Pumpkin Pie

I could eat a slice of pumpkin pie every day for the month of November and never get tired of it. This pie is sweetened with both brown and granulated sugar plus just a little bit of sorghum, which adds a richness without being overly sweet. For the past several years, I've roasted pumpkins and frozen them to make pies and bread with. It's a bit extra, but I enjoy the process. Canned pumpkin, as long as it isn't seasoned, is fine, too. But if you can get some sugar pumpkins, also called pie pumpkins, at the grocery store, give them a try. If you really plan ahead, you can grow your own. I like to use my All-Butter Pie Dough (page 71) for this. I take the scraps of the dough and roll them out to hand-cut leaves and a pumpkin to bake off and then decorate it when it cools. This recipe makes enough for a 9-inch (23 cm) deep dish pie or two 8-inch (20 cm) regular pies.

YIELD 8 Servings | **SEASONS ENJOYED** Fall, winter

- ½ cup (110 g) packed light brown sugar
- ¼ cup (50 g) granulated sugar
- 2 tablespoons sorghum
- ½ teaspoon salt
- 1 tablespoon plain flour
- ½ teaspoon ground cinnamon
- ¼ teaspoon ground nutmeg
- ¼ teaspoon ground allspice
- ⅛ teaspoon ground cloves
- 3 large eggs
- 2 cups (480 ml) homemade pumpkin puree or 1 can (15 ounces/425 g) pumpkin puree
- 1 can (12 ounces/354 ml) evaporated milk
- ½ recipe All-Butter Pie Dough (page 71)

1 Preheat the oven to 450°F (230°C/gas 8).

2 In a large bowl, add the brown sugar, granulated sugar, sorghum, salt, flour, cinnamon, nutmeg, allspice, and cloves; whisk until smooth. Whisk in the eggs, pumpkin puree, and evaporated milk.

3 Roll out the pie dough about 1½ inches (4 cm) beyond the size of the pie dish (or dishes) you're using, and fit it into the bottom. Add the filling.

4 Bake for 10 minutes, then adjust the oven control to 350°F (175°C/gas 4). Continue to bake until the filling is cooked but still has a slight jiggle and a knife inserted into the center comes out clean, 45 to 50 minutes.

5 Cool completely before serving, about 1 hour. While it cools, use the scraps of leftover dough to cut out and bake off, just like you do for a blind-baked crust (see page 71)—leaves, pumpkins, or any other shape you would like—and use them to decorate the cooled pie. Serve with a dollop of freshly whipped cream.

I RECKON YOU COULD

Make homemade pumpkin puree: Preheat the oven to 350°F (175°C/gas 4). Remove the stem, cut the pumpkin in half from stem to bottom end, and scoop out the seeds. Place the pumpkin halves cut side down on a parchment-lined baking sheet. With a sharp knife, cut a couple of slits in each half. Bake until easily pierced with a fork, 50 minutes to 1 hour. Let cool to the touch, about 30 minutes. Pull the skin off and remove any parts that are fibrous or hard. The flesh can then be pureed in a food processor or blender. Portion it into cups in freezer bags so you know how much you have; press all the air out and freeze for up to 1 year.

Pineapple Pound Cake

Pound cakes have always been popular because they're so versatile. I bake mine in my vintage cast-iron fluted cake pan from the 1950s. I love it because it gives a perfect golden brown on the outside of the cake. Once cast iron heats up, it stays warm for a very long time, so it bakes cakes very evenly, even if your oven has cold spots. If you don't have a fluted cake pan, you can use two 9-inch (23 cm) loaf pans, following the same directions to bake. When I was going through my grandmaw's recipes, I found her handwritten recipe card for Pineapple Pound Cake. I've made this several times, and the edges come out just a little crunchy when it's first baked—those edges are so good!

YIELD 10 to 12 servings | **SEASONS ENJOYED** Spring, summer, fall, winter

Shortening or Cake Goop (page 21), for greasing

2 cups (240 g) plain flour

2 cups (400 g) sugar

1 teaspoon salt

1 teaspoon baking soda

3 large eggs

1 cup (240 ml) vegetable oil

1 teaspoon vanilla extract

1 can (20 ounces/567 g) crushed pineapple, drained

1 Preheat the oven to 350°F (175°C/gas 4). Grease a 9½-inch (24 cm) fluted baking pan with shortening and lightly dust it with flour, or use Cake Goop.

2 In the bowl of a stand mixer fitted with the paddle attachment, stir together the flour, sugar, salt, and baking soda. Add the eggs, oil, and vanilla and mix at medium speed until a thick batter forms, 2 to 3 minutes. Fold in the crushed pineapple; the batter will loosen up a bit from the pineapple's juices.

3 Transfer the batter to the prepared baking pan. Bake until a cake tester inserted in the center comes out clean, 50 to 60 minutes.

4 Transfer to a wire rack to cool for 10 minutes, then place the cooling rack upside down on top of the pan and invert to turn it out. Let cool completely, about 30 minutes. Serve with a simple sugar glaze drizzled over it, a dusting of powdered sugar, or with a scoop of vanilla ice cream on the side.

Cranberry Orange Pound Cake

My brothers were all in FFA (Future Farmers of America) in high school, and their fundraiser each year was selling cases of navel oranges. Mom would always get a case and store what she could in the crisper drawer while the rest went in the crawl space under the house. They stayed nice and cold there. It was such a treat in the evenings when she would get us an orange. We'd roll them, pressing down hard, to loosen all the juice. Then she'd cut a hole in the top and we'd suck on them until we got every last drop out. These were the original juice boxes. Then we'd peel 'em and eat what was left.

YIELD 10 to 12 servings | **SEASON ENJOYED** Winter

Shortening or Cake Goop (page 21), for greasing

1 cup (2 sticks/205 g) salted butter, at room temperature

2½ cups (500 g) granulated sugar

4 large eggs, at room temperature

Grated zest and juice of 1 orange, plus more for garnish (optional)

¾ cup (180 ml) whole-milk buttermilk or enough to equal 1 cup (240 ml) when mixed with the orange juice

3 cups (360 g) plain flour

1 teaspoon baking powder

½ teaspoon salt

1 bag (11 ounces/312 g) fresh or frozen cranberries

Powdered sugar, for dusting

I RECKON YOU COULD

For a festive presentation when serving, slice the cake and arrange on a platter with some fresh orange slices, sugared cranberries, and some freshly whipped cream garnished with a little orange zest.

1 Preheat the oven to 325°F (165°C/gas 3). Grease a 9½-inch (24 cm) fluted baking pan or two 9-inch (23 cm) loaf pans with shortening and lightly dust with flour, or use Cake Goop.

2 In the bowl of a stand mixer fitted with the paddle attachment, beat the butter and sugar at medium speed until light and fluffy, 4 to 5 minutes. With the mixer at low speed, add 1 egg at a time, mixing until fully incorporated. Add the orange zest and juice and the buttermilk and mix until fully incorporated.

3 In a medium bowl, sift together the flour, baking powder, and salt. With the mixer at medium speed, spoon in the flour mixture, a little at a time, until fully incorporated, 2 to 3 minutes. Reserve a few cranberries for garnish, then gently fold in the remaining cranberries.

4 Transfer the batter to the prepared baking pan and bake until a cake tester inserted in the center comes out clean, about 1 hour and 30 minutes.

5 Transfer to a wire rack to cool for 10 minutes, then place the cooling rack upside down on top of the pan and invert to turn it out. Let cool completely, about 30 minutes. If desired, squeeze a bit of juice from an orange over the top before dusting with the powdered sugar. Garnish with fresh cranberries and, if using, a little orange zest.

Christmas Crisp

I love mincemeat pie, and so did my granddaddy. Grandmaw would make it, and I couldn't wait for a slice when we spent Christmas at their house. I don't know if she ever made the mincemeat from scratch, but I buy it in a jar from a local Amish market (one day I'll make it). This crisp reminds me of those Christmases. I love using Cosmic Crisp apples for baking. They don't brown when you cut them, they hold their shape well, and are tender, not mushy, when baked.

YIELD 8 servings | **SEASON ENJOYED** Winter

Filling

3 cups (480 g) peeled, chopped apples
2 cups (200 g) fresh or frozen cranberries
Grated zest and juice of 1 orange
¾ cup (165 g) packed light brown sugar
1 teaspoon ground cinnamon
½ teaspoon ground nutmeg
¼ teaspoon ground cloves
2 tablespoons cornstarch

Crisp Topping

1 cup (89 g) rolled oats
⅔ cup (80 g) plain flour
⅔ cup (145 g) packed light brown sugar
Dash salt
½ cup (1 stick/115 g) cold salted butter, cubed
4 heaping tablespoons prepared mincemeat

1 Preheat the oven to 350°F (175°C/gas 4).

2 Make the filling: In a large bowl, add the apples, cranberries, orange zest, and juice and toss to combine; let sit for about 10 minutes. Add the brown sugar, cinnamon, nutmeg, cloves, and cornstarch; toss to coat well and transfer to a 9-inch (23 cm) round, 3-inch-deep (7.5 cm) baking dish.

3 Make the crisp topping: In a food processor, add the oats, flour, brown sugar, and salt; give it a pulse to mix. Add the cubed butter and pulse until the butter is incorporated and the mixture looks like coarse meal. Add the mincemeat and pulse just 2 to 3 times to combine. The mixture should be crumbly. Spoon it over the apple filling.

4 Bake until the crisp is golden, about 45 minutes. Let cool for 15 minutes before serving. Serve plain or with cream, whipped cream, or vanilla ice cream.

Brownies

Mick said his mom made the best brownies. She gave me her recipe, and they're honestly the best I've ever made. You won't ever try a box mix again. When the brownies cool, they fall slightly in the middle, making them dense and fudgy. Her recipe just called for all regular cocoa, but I added the dark, and it makes them so rich and delicious. This originally called for jumbo eggs, I think because that's what she always bought, but I've adapted it to use large eggs.

YIELD 9 to 12 brownies | **SEASONS ENJOYED** Spring, summer, fall, winter

1¼ cups (250 g) sugar
¾ cup (95 g) self-rising flour
⅛ teaspoon salt
⅓ cup (30 g) regular unsweetened cocoa powder
2 tablespoons dark unsweetened cocoa powder
½ cup (1 stick/115 g) salted butter, melted
3 large eggs

1 Preheat the oven to 350°F (175°C/gas 4). Grease an 8-inch (20 cm) square baking dish with cooking spray or line it with parchment paper.

2 In a large bowl, sift together the sugar, flour, salt, regular cocoa, and dark cocoa. Add the melted butter and eggs; stir until smooth. The batter will be stiff. Transfer to the baking dish and spread all the way to the edges and corners.

3 Bake until the middle no longer jiggles, 22 to 25 minutes. Let cool for 10 minutes. Cut into squares and serve with a large glass of cold milk.

Belsnickeling in the Shenandoah Valley was a tradition up into the 1940s. Photo Courtesy of Rocktown History, Dayton, Virginia.

The Appalachian Lore of the Belsnickel

For over half a century in the late 1800s and early 1900s in Appalachia, children feared and anticipated a visit from the Belsnickel. He would show up just after dark in the weeks leading up to Christmas dressed in furs and carrying a switch. Holding candy in one pocket and lumps of coal in the other, he would come to see the kids of the house. One by one he'd ask them if they'd been good, to which they had to answer honestly or their parents would let him know the truth. If they were honest, he'd give them a treat, but if not, they would get a lump of coal and probably a switch. They believed that the Belsnickel reported back to Santa, and if it was a bad report, they wouldn't have a good Christmas. When he arrived, the whole family wanted him to feel welcome and enjoy his visit so they'd all have a good Christmas. The women of the house would lay out a spread of cakes and cookies, while the men would offer up something to drink. In Appalachia, that was often moonshine or homemade wine. By the end of the evening, depending on how many houses the Belsnickel (who you might have guessed was usually a neighbor) visited, he might or might not make it back home before dawn. I like to think that's how the tradition of an open house during the holidays began. This tradition changed over time: You might have a group of Belsnickelers showing up at your door wearing masks and tattered clothes. They might sing or perform for you in hopes of getting a treat before heading to the next house. And the household would make a game of it to try and figure out who was behind the masks. This is where the tradition of caroling came from, as well as trick-or-treating throughout Appalachia.

Christmas may be on December 25th, but back then in parts of Appalachia they still celebrated Old Christmas on January 6th. It was a tradition carried over from a couple of centuries prior, back in the old country (England, Scotland, and Ireland for the most part), where they still followed the Julian calendar. This is where we get the song "The Twelve Days of Christmas," with day one being on December 25th and the twelfth day on January 6th.

Around Christmas, Mary from next door would tell me how she missed Belsnickeling. She would laugh as she recalled her brothers dressing up and going door-to-door. She said they looked awful! They'd dress up in dirty clothes, torn and worn, with black all over their faces or a sack over their head with a face painted on it, and carrying a stick or a whip. Then they'd go from one neighbor's house to the next. Since they helped their dad make moonshine, I think they may have carried their own, and by the time they made it back home, they'd sometimes pass out in the yard. If they made it to the porch, Mary would help them get to their beds.

As much as Mary loved Christmas, I think she had more fun on Halloween. She would count how many kids they'd have each year and loved trying to figure out who they were behind their costumes. With their getups changing and the kids growing, it was always challenging. She'd laugh and cover her face as they revealed themselves. She lived into her late eighties and looked forward to it more each year.

Belsnickeling was a ritual up into the 1940s in the mountains of Virginia, where it may have been the last stronghold of the tradition throughout Appalachia. Many folks I mention this to today have never heard of it. I chuckle when I see an old stuffed Santa with a scary look on his face, because I know that he's really showing us how Belsnickel became Santa over the decades, and now we see him as a jolly old elf.

Belsnickel Cookies

These cookies are closely connected to the traditional sugar cookie that we all make during Christmas, as both traditions originated out of Central Appalachia during the holidays. The dough for these is very soft and tender, so work quickly when you roll it out to keep it from getting too warm, and keep your counter well-floured to keep it from sticking.

YIELD 3 to 4 dozen cookies | **SEASON ENJOYED** Winter

1 cup (2 sticks/225 g) salted butter, softened

2 cups (400 g) sugar, plus more for sprinkling

4 large eggs

3½ cups (420 g) plain flour, plus more for dusting

1 teaspoon baking soda

Pinch of salt

I RECKON YOU COULD
For an authentic Belsnickel cookie, you simply use additional granulated sugar on top to decorate them, but why not add some festive colored sugars, coarse sugars, or decorative sprinkles, letting the kids help decorate. It adds to the fun!

1 In a large bowl, add the butter and sugar and beat with a wooden spoon until light and fluffy. Add the eggs and stir until well incorporated.

2 In a separate medium bowl, sift together the flour, baking soda, and salt. Add to the butter mixture and stir until all the flour is incorporated. Cover and chill in the refrigerator for 1 hour or overnight.

3 Preheat the oven to 350°F (175°C/gas 4). Line a baking sheet with parchment paper.

4 On a well-floured surface, divide the dough into 4 equal portions. Using a well-floured rolling pin, roll out one portion of the dough to about ¼-inch (6 mm) thickness (store the remaining dough in the refrigerator until needed). Cut with a biscuit cutter or cookie cutter. The dough can soften while you're working with it so, using a spatula, gently lift the cut cookies and place them on the prepared baking sheet, spacing them about 2 inches (5 cm) apart. Sprinkle additional sugar on top of each cookie.

5 Bake until lightly golden, 12 to 14 minutes. Allow to cool on the baking sheet until set, about 10 minutes. Transfer the cookies to a wire rack until completely cooled, about 20 minutes. Store in an airtight container for up to 1 week.

Three-Way Shortbread

While going through my Grandmaw Edge's recipe box, I found so many recipes and notes that intrigued me. One was for her Three-Way Shortbread. I recognized her handwriting right away. It's a simple recipe that tells you how to make it into wedges and how to make thumbprints, but there's not a third recipe! I decided that meant I was supposed to add the last to make the recipe card complete.

YIELD 12 to 16 wedges/thumbprint cookies | **SEASONS ENJOYED** Spring, summer, fall, winter

½ cup (1 stick/115 g) salted butter, softened
¼ cup (50 g) sugar
1¼ cups (150 g) plain flour, plus more for dusting
Jam or preserves of choice, for thumbprints

1 Preheat the oven to 325°F (165°C/gas 3).

2 Make the dough: In a large bowl, beat the butter and sugar until light and fluffy, then gradually add the flour and stir until crumbly. Form it into a ball and knead just until smooth, 1 to 2 minutes.

3 To make wedges: On a lightly floured surface, using a lightly floured rolling pin, roll out the shortbread dough into an 8-inch (20 cm) circle. Transfer the dough onto a parchment-lined baking sheet. Using a sharp knife, cut the dough into 12 or 16 wedges; do not separate the pieces. Bake until the edges just begin to brown, 25 to 30 minutes. While they're still warm from the oven, recut the wedges. Let cool completely, about 20 minutes. Store in an airtight container for up to 2 weeks.

4 To make thumbprints: Line a baking sheet with parchment paper. Using a tablespoon, scoop the dough and roll them into 12 to 16 balls; place them on the prepared baking sheet about 2 inches (5 cm) apart. Make an indention with your thumb in the center of each one. Bake until the bottoms are golden brown, about 18 minutes. Remove from the oven and place ½ teaspoon of preserves in each thumbprint. Let them cool on the baking sheet for 10 minutes, then transfer to a wire rack to cool completely, about 10 minutes. Store in an airtight container for up to 2 weeks.

FINDING MY OWN WAY

I asked my aunt if she knew what the third way was supposed to be for Grandmaw's recipe, and she had no idea. I used a similar recipe to teach a kid's baking class and had leftover dough that I took home that evening. That shortbread recipe was a riddle for the kids to figure out. It goes:

Half as much sugar as butter
Twice as much flour as butter
2 cups of flour gets a teaspoon of salt

I thought about making a cobbler that weekend for my mother-in-law—blackberry is her favorite—and I decided to use the leftover dough as a crumble topping. It was perfect. I'd found my own third way! I've also made this with blueberries and peaches, and it works equally as well. Just find your favorite cobbler recipe that calls for a dough topping instead of a batter, and give it a try.

Mick's Banana Pudding

When he was growing up, Mick's mom always made banana pudding from scratch for holidays and get-togethers. After his Mamaw passed away, those get-togethers dwindled, and she stopped making it. Mick picked up the tradition, and now he makes one for all the family gatherings. When he looks for bananas to buy, he gets the greenest he can if it will be a few days before he's going to make it. They have to be just ripe, and not spotted or bruised. When making it, Mick prefers it to sit in the refrigerator overnight so the pudding is completely set, but if you need it that day, try to give it at least four hours in the refrigerator.

YIELD 10 to 12 servings | **SEASONS ENJOYED** Spring, summer, fall, winter

1 cup (200 g) sugar
5 tablespoons cornstarch
4 cups (960 ml) whole milk
5 large egg yolks
1 teaspoon vanilla extract
¼ cup (½ stick/55 g) salted butter
4 or 5 bananas, cut crosswise into ½-inch-thick (12 mm) slices
1 box (12 ounces/340 g) vanilla wafers
1 tub (8 ounces/227 g) whipped topping (such as Cool Whip)

1 In a 2- to 3-quart (2 to 3 L) saucepan over medium heat, stir together the sugar and cornstarch, then slowly whisk in the milk. Cook, whisking constantly, until it begins to steam and thicken, 5 to 6 minutes.

2 In a large measuring cup, beat the egg yolks, then, while still whisking the eggs, slowly stream in ½ cup (120 ml) of the hot milk mixture to temper them. While vigorously whisking the milk mixture, slowly stream the tempered egg yolks into the milk. Continue to whisk until thick, about 5 to 6 minutes.

3 Remove from the heat and stir in the vanilla and butter. Let it cool, stirring every few minutes to keep a skin from forming over the top; cooling at room temperature can take up to 1 hour. To speed this up, you can set the pan in a bowl of ice, stirring the pudding every few minutes.

4 In a 9 x 13-inch (23 to 33 cm) baking dish, spread a third of the pudding; add a layer of banana slices, then a layer of vanilla wafers. Repeat, then finish with a layer of pudding. Top it off with a layer of whipped topping, covering it completely. Cover and refrigerate for 4 hours to overnight before serving.

Snow Cream

This may be the reason this cookbook has come to life. During a snowstorm in January of 2024, I decided to make some snow cream and put up a reel about it. I didn't think much of it, because I've been eating snow cream all my life. Within hours it had hundreds, then thousands of plays. The next day, it was close to one million, and within a week, it was at more than thirty million. It's been played more than thirty-six million times with a total play time of twenty-eight years—yes, years! This is a recipe that you just make, there are no exact measurements. You just have to go for it. So here's what I do.

YIELD 6 to 8 servings | **SEASON ENJOYED** Winter

6 quarts (5.7 L) clean fresh snow
¾ to 1 cup (150 to 200 g) sugar
1 can (12 ounces/354 ml) evaporated milk
1 to 2 teaspoons vanilla extract

1 Gather snow from clean surfaces, but only after it's been snowing for a couple of hours if it's the first snow of the season.

2 Fill a 6-quart (6 L) bowl or saucepan to heaping with the snow and add the sugar, about half the can of evaporated milk, and vanilla. Stir to combine and add more evaporated milk as needed to make it creamy, but still thick.

3 Serve immediately.

4 Make a reel about it and don't look at the comments. People can be mean.

5 Wait for a couple of publishers to contact you about writing a cookbook.

6 Become a famous cookbook author.

7 Stay humble by still making your own snow cream.

Peanut Brittle

When I was a kid, there wasn't a holiday at Grandmaw Barton's that she didn't have boxes of peanut brittle on the table. It was her favorite candy, so everyone got her some. Had I known then how easy it was to make, I would have given her some homemade. When I was going through my other grandmaw's recipes, I found this gem. Each time I've made it, I give some away. And each time, I'm told it's the best peanut brittle they've ever had. I think one secret is using raw peanuts. Roasted and salted peanuts will alter the taste. Unless you can find them shelled raw, you'll probably have to shell them yourself, but trust me, it is worth the effort. I have found that a 1½-pound (680 g) bag of raw peanuts in the shells yields me the quart (600 g) of peanuts I need.

Notes on making brittle: My grandmaw's recipe said to cook on high for 20 minutes, and that the syrup will darken when it's done. I found that medium-high heat works well, and I use a candy thermometer to make sure the mixture is between 300 and 310°F (149 to 154°C). I also stir mine very gently with a wooden spoon, being careful not to let the spoon touch the sides or splash any syrup onto the sides of the pot (to prevent it from burning). You have to work quickly once it reaches temperature, so have the baking soda measured out and the baking sheet buttered beforehand. When ready, pour it across the entire length of the pan and very gently spread it out. You want it to be light and airy; applying too much pressure can push out the air bubbles and make it very hard when it cools.

YIELD 2 pounds (907 g) | **SEASON ENJOYED** Winter

- 2 tablespoons salted butter, softened, plus more for greasing
- 2 cups (400 g) granulated sugar
- 4 cups (600 g) shelled raw peanuts
- 1 cup (240 ml) light corn syrup
- 2 teaspoons baking soda

1 Liberally grease a 10 x 15-inch (25 x 38 cm) or larger baking dish with butter.

2 In a medium (3-quart/3-L) saucepan over medium-high heat, combine the butter, sugar, peanuts, and corn syrup. Stir gently with a wooden spoon until the sugar dissolves. Heat to boiling, and cook, stirring occasionally (gently, and just in the center), until it reaches 300 to 310°F (149 to 154°C), about 20 minutes. The syrup and peanuts will darken a little as it gets close to being done. (When stirring, make sure not to touch the sides of the pot, to prevent any peanuts from burning.) Remove from the heat and immediately stir in the baking soda. It will foam up to almost double in size and turn much lighter in color.

3 Pour the brittle into the prepared pan and gently spread it out. Allow it to cool completely, about 30 minutes.

4 Break it up into pieces right in the pan, then store the pieces in an airtight container for up to a month.

Christmas Fudge

Mick's mom always made fudge at Christmas, but as they all grew up and moved on, she stopped making it; because of all the stirring, it became hard on her hands. Mick asked me a few years ago if I could make it. I tried a version of my own, but he said, "It ain't Mom's. Hers is firm." So, I asked her for the recipe, and she gave me her whole cookbook. When I found the fudge recipe, it had notes on the side, lines through the middle, and things scribbled out. Over the years she'd perfected it, so without her notes, there's no way I could have made it as good as hers. He said she always used the same round aluminum pie pan to make it, year after year. He remembered that specifically because it was the only aluminum pan she had, and it was just for her fudge. Somehow, she made a disposable aluminum pan last for twenty years. Now that's Appalachian right there.

YIELD 64 squares | **SEASON ENJOYED** Winter

¾ cup (180 ml) whole milk
2 ounces (57 g) unsweetened baking chocolate
2 cups (400 g) sugar
Pinch of salt
2 tablespoons salted butter, plus more for greasing
1 teaspoon vanilla extract
½ cup (120 ml) smooth peanut butter

1 In a small heavy-bottomed saucepan, warm the milk and chocolate over low heat, stirring until fully incorporated. Increase the heat to medium, add the sugar and salt and stir continuously until dissolved. Heat to boiling and cook, without stirring, until it reaches 235 to 240°F (113 to 116°C). If you don't have a candy thermometer, you can check by dropping a little drip of the mixture into a glass of cold water. It will form a soft ball if it's done. Remove from the heat and stir in the butter, vanilla, and peanut butter. Let it cool to lukewarm, about 20 minutes.

2 Grease an 8-inch (20 cm) square pan.

3 Beat the fudge with a wooden spoon until it loses its shine, then immediately spread it into an even layer in the prepared pan. Let cool completely, about 1 hour before cutting into 1-inch (2.5 cm) squares. Store in an airtight container for up to 2 weeks.

Peanut Butter Fudge

When I was going through family recipes to pull what I wanted to include, I found a card in Mom's handwriting, tucked inside an old cookbook, for peanut butter fudge. I'd forgotten that she even made it until I came across this. Peanut butter was easily her favorite thing to eat. I remember her saying that when she was pregnant, she craved it all the time and could eat an entire jar in a weekend. So, I've probably been enjoying this fudge since before I was even born! This is a soft, creamy fudge that just melts in your mouth!

YIELD About 120 squares | **SEASONS ENJOYED** Spring, summer, fall, winter

3 tablespoons salted butter
3 cups (600 g) sugar
2 tablespoons corn syrup, light or dark
¾ cup (180 ml) whole milk
1 cup (240 ml) peanut butter, smooth or crunchy
1 tablespoon vanilla extract

1 Grease two 8-inch (20 cm) square pans or one 9 x 13-inch (23 by 33 cm) pan with butter.

2 In a 3-quart (3 L) saucepan, whisk together the butter, sugar, corn syrup, and milk. Heat to boiling over medium-high heat, then reduce the heat to medium-low and continue to cook, without stirring, until it reaches 235 to 240°F (113 to 116°C). If you don't have a candy thermometer, you can check by dropping a little drip of the mixture into a glass of cold water. It will form a soft ball if it's done. Remove from the heat and stir in the peanut butter and vanilla, then immediately pour into the prepared dish (or dishes). Let cool completely, about 1½ to 2 hours, before cutting into 1-inch (2.5 cm) squares. Store in an airtight container for up to 2 weeks.

Final Thoughts

If I could have forever, I would spend it with everyone I've ever known and loved coming to the table, lots of food passed around, lots of laughs, and memories being told and retold.

So when time is no longer a constraint, life is no longer a ritual of responsibility, and forever is a heaven of your own making, you'll know where to find me.

Acknowledgments

To Granddaddy and Grandmaw Barton, Granddaddy and Grandmaw Edge, Harry and Barbara (my parents), and Mary and Charlie and MaryAnn (my neighbors growing up). You made me who I am. Without you, I would not know what it means to be Appalachian.

To Aunt Alice, my dad's younger sister. She's shared with me all of Grandmaw's recipes, told me countless stories, shared her own recipes, and gifted me my Grandmaw's favorite china, which you'll see throughout the book.

To my husband, Mick, who's always messin' and gommin'. You make me who I am. You were the first to believe me years ago when I said I was gonna write a book. You encourage me to realize my potential, and will always be my first taste-tester, but never my only or last. I have no idea what you're trying to say sometimes!

About the Author

Jimmy Proffitt is a freelance writer and passionate home cook who grew up in the Shenandoah Valley of Virginia. He started his blog, *The Appalachian Tale*, several years ago as a creative outlet to write about growing up Appalachian and share stories of family recipes. He's written for various print and digital publications and received a Taste50 Award from Taste of the South magazine in 2022. He is also a member of IACP, the International Association of Culinary Professionals, earning a Member of the Year Award in 2023. He lives in East Tennessee with his husband, dogs, and cats. This is his first cookbook, but he says it won't be his last.

Index

A

apple cider: Baked Country Ham, 91
apples
- Apple Cinnamon Biscuits, 41
- Christmas Crisp, 166
- Christmas Morning Biscuits, 45
- Homemade Applesauce, 77
- Overnight Slow Cooker Apple Butter, 75
- Roast Turkey, 84

artichoke hearts: Bacon Spinach Artichoke Dip, 132

B

bacon
- Bacon Spinach Artichoke Dip, 132
- Mick's Baked Beans, 114
- Pennies, Dollars, and Gold Potpie, 99–100

bacon grease
- Appalachian Skillet Cornbread Dressing, 117
- Green Tomato Onion Cornbread, 64
- Leather Britches, 123

bananas: Mick's Banana Pudding, 176
barbecue sauce: Mom's Meatloaf, 87
beans
- Garden Medley Pickles, 29
- Leather Britches, 120–121, 123
- Marinated Bean Salad, 113
- Mick's Baked Beans, 114
- Spicy Dilly Beans, 32

beef
- Grandmaw's West Virginia Hot Dog Chili Sauce, 78
- Mick's Baked Beans, 114
- Mom's Meatloaf, 87
- Sloppy Joes, 97

beef broth
- Grandmaw's West Virginia Hot Dog Chili Sauce, 78
- Oyster Mushroom Sauce, 81
- Pot Roast Gravy, 50

bell peppers
- Garden Medley Pickles, 29
- Grandmaw's West Virginia Hot Dog Chili Sauce, 78
- Hushpuppies, 101–102
- Marinated Bean Salad, 113
- Sloppy Joes, 97

Belsnickeling, 171
beverages
- Christmas Eve Eggnog, 140
- Punch for 50, 143
- Sweet Tea, 139
- Triple-Chocolate Hot Cocoa Mix, 144

biscuits. See also breads; rolls
- Apple Cinnamon Biscuits, 41
- Biscuit Dough Crackers, 136
- Christmas Morning Biscuits, 45
- Drop Biscuits, 42
- Flaky Layers Buttermilk Biscuits, 38
- tips, 37

black-eyed peas: Pennies, Dollars, and Gold Potpie, 99–100
bourbon: Oyster Mushroom Sauce, 81
breads. See also biscuits; rolls
- Bloody Butcher Cornbread, 63
- Brown Butter Cornbread, 60
- Fluffy Buttermilk Pancakes, 68
- Green Tomato Onion Cornbread, 64
- Hot Water Cornbread, 67
- Hushpuppies, 101–102
- Pone Bread, 46
- tips, 55
- Zucchini Bread, 153

bread crumbs
- Appalachian Skillet Cornbread Dressing, 117
- Mom's Meatloaf, 87

brownies: Brownies, 169
butter crackers: Grandmaw's Baked Squash, 118

C

cabbage: Coleslaw, 110
cakes
- Cranberry Orange Pound Cake, 165
- Pineapple Pound Cake, 162
- Pineapple Upside-Down Cake, 154
- Triple-Layer Carrot Cake, 149, 150
- Zucchini Bread, 153

carrots
- Garden Medley Pickles, 29
- Pennies, Dollars, and Gold Potpie, 99–100
- Roast Turkey, 84
- Triple-Layer Carrot Cake, 150

catfish: RB's Fish Fry and Hushpuppies, 101–102
cauliflower: Garden Medley Pickles, 29
celery
- Marinated Bean Salad, 113
- Pennies, Dollars, and Gold Potpie, 99–100
- Roast Turkey, 84

cheddar cheese
- Bacon Spinach Artichoke Dip, 132
- Sausage Balls, 131

cherries
- Pineapple Upside-Down Cake, 154
- Quick Cherry Sauce, 77

chicken
- Cilantro Lime Chicken Wings, 135
- Dad's BBQ Chicken, 94

chicken broth: Oyster Mushroom Sauce, 81
chicken soup: Grandmaw's Baked Squash, 118
chocolate
- Appalachian Chocolate Gravy, 52
- Christmas Fudge, 183
- Peanut Butter Fudge, 184
- Triple-Chocolate Hot Cocoa Mix, 144

cinnamon
- Appalachian Pumpkin Pie, 161
- Apple Cinnamon Biscuits, 41
- Christmas Crisp, 166
- Christmas Eve Eggnog, 140
- Christmas Morning Biscuits, 45
- Green Tomato Pie, 158
- Mock Apple Pie, 157
- Orange Cinnamon Butter, 45
- Overnight Slow Cooker Apple Butter, 75
- Triple-Layer Carrot Cake, 150
- Zucchini Bread, 153

cocoa powder
- Appalachian Chocolate Gravy, 52
- Brownies, 169
- Triple-Chocolate Hot Cocoa Mix, 144

coconut: Triple-Layer Carrot Cake, 150
collard greens: Pennies, Dollars, and Gold Potpie, 99–100
cookies
- Belsnickel Cookies, 172
- Three-Way Shortbread, 175

corn: Pennies, Dollars, and Gold Potpie, 99–100
cornbread
- Appalachian Skillet Cornbread Dressing, 117
- Bloody Butcher Cornbread, 63
- Brown Butter Cornbread, 60
- Green Tomato Onion Cornbread, 64
- Hot Water Cornbread, 67

cornmeal
- Bloody Butcher Cornbread, 63
- Brown Butter Cornbread, 60
- Green Tomato Onion Cornbread, 64
- Hot Water Cornbread, 67
- Hushpuppies, 101–102

Pennies, Dollars, and Gold Potpie, 99–100
RB's Fish Fry and Hushpuppies, 101–102
crackers: Biscuit Dough Crackers, 136
cranberries
Christmas Crisp, 166
Christmas Morning Biscuits, 45
Cranberry Glaze, 45
Cranberry Orange Pound Cake, 165
cream cheese
Bacon Spinach Artichoke Dip, 132
Sausage Balls, 131
Triple-Layer Carrot Cake, 150
cream of chicken soup: Grandmaw's Baked Squash, 118
cucumbers
Bread-and-Butter Pickles, 26
Dill Pickles, 28
Garden Medley Pickles, 29
Refrigerator Pickles, 33

D

dip: Bacon Spinach Artichoke Dip, 132
dressing
Appalachian Skillet Cornbread Dressing, 117
Spring Salad Dressing, 80

E

eggs
Appalachian Pumpkin Pie, 161
Belsnickel Cookies, 172
Bloody Butcher Cornbread, 63
Brown Butter Cornbread, 60
Brownies, 169
Christmas Eve Eggnog, 140
Cranberry Orange Pound Cake, 165
Deviled Eggs, 106
Fluffy Buttermilk Pancakes, 68
Golden Potato Salad, 109
Grandmaw's Baked Squash, 118
Grandmaw's Refrigerator Rolls, 56–57
Green Tomato Onion Cornbread, 64
Green Tomato Pie, 158
Hushpuppies, 101–102
Mick's Banana Pudding, 176
Mom's Meatloaf, 87
Pennies, Dollars, and Gold Potpie, 99–100
Pineapple Pound Cake, 162
Pineapple Upside-Down Cake, 154
Pone Bread, 46
Triple-Layer Carrot Cake, 150
Zucchini Bread, 153

F

fish: RB's Fish Fry and Hushpuppies, 101–102
fudge
Christmas Fudge, 183
Peanut Butter Fudge, 184

G

garlic
Appalachian Skillet Cornbread Dressing, 117
Bacon Spinach Artichoke Dip, 132
Dill Pickles, 28
Garden Medley Pickles, 29
Grandmaw's West Virginia Hot Dog Chili Sauce, 78
Leather Britches, 123
Mick's Baked Beans, 114
Mom's Meatloaf, 87
Refrigerator Pickles, 33
Sloppy Joes, 97
Spicy Dilly Beans, 32
ginger ale: Punch for 50, 143
gravy
Appalachian Chocolate Gravy, 52
Pan Gravy, 53
Pot Roast Gravy, 50
Sausage Patties with Gravy, 49
tips, 48
great northern beans: Marinated Bean Salad, 113
green beans
Garden Medley Pickles, 29
Leather Britches, 123
Marinated Bean Salad, 113
Spicy Dilly Beans, 32

H

ham
Baked Country Ham, 91
Boiled Country Ham, 90
Leather Britches, 123
tips, 88
honey
Dad's BBQ Chicken, 94
Overnight Slow Cooker Apple Butter, 75
hot peppers: Refrigerator Pickles, 33

K

ketchup
Mick's Baked Beans, 114
Mom's Meatloaf, 87
kidney beans: Marinated Bean Salad, 113

L

lemon
Dad's BBQ Chicken, 94
Mock Apple Pie, 157
lime: Cilantro Lime Chicken Wings, 135

M

mayonnaise
Bacon Spinach Artichoke Dip, 132
Coleslaw, 110
Deviled Eggs, 106
Golden Potato Salad, 109
Grandmaw's Baked Squash, 118
Spring Salad Dressing, 80
mincemeat: Christmas Crisp, 166
molasses
Baked Country Ham, 91
Boiled Country Ham, 90
mozzarella cheese: Bacon Spinach Artichoke Dip, 132
mushrooms: Oyster Mushroom Sauce, 81
mustard
Deviled Eggs, 106
Golden Potato Salad, 109
Mick's Baked Beans, 114
Mom's Meatloaf, 87

O

oats: Christmas Crisp, 166
okra: Pickled Okra, 31
onions
Appalachian Skillet Cornbread Dressing, 117
Bread-and-Butter Pickles, 26
Garden Medley Pickles, 29
Golden Potato Salad, 109
Grandmaw's Baked Squash, 118
Grandmaw's West Virginia Hot Dog Chili Sauce, 78
Green Tomato Onion Cornbread, 64
Green Tomato Pickles, 30
Hushpuppies, 101–102
Leather Britches, 123
Marinated Bean Salad, 113
Mom's Meatloaf, 87

Roast Turkey, 84
Sloppy Joes, 97
Squash Pickles, 27
onion soup mix: Mick's Baked Beans, 114
orange
Baked Country Ham, 91
Christmas Crisp, 166
Christmas Morning Biscuits, 45
Cranberry Orange Pound Cake, 165
Orange Cinnamon Butter, 45
Orange Sugar, 45
Punch for 50, 143

P

pancakes: Fluffy Buttermilk Pancakes, 68
Parmesan cheese: Bacon Spinach Artichoke Dip, 132
peanuts
Christmas Fudge, 183
Peanut Brittle, 180
Peanut Butter Fudge, 184
pecans: Triple-Layer Carrot Cake, 150
peppercorns
Dill Pickles, 28
Garden Medley Pickles, 29
Green Tomato Pickles, 30
Refrigerator Pickles, 33
Roast Turkey, 84
pepperoni: Grandmaw's Pepperoni Rolls, 127, 128
peppers, red
Pickled Okra, 31
Spicy Dilly Beans, 32
pickles
Bread-and-Butter Pickles, 26
Dill Pickles, 28
Garden Medley Pickles, 29
Golden Potato Salad, 109
Green Tomato Pickles, 30
Pickled Okra, 31
Refrigerator Pickles, 33
Spicy Dilly Beans, 32
Squash Pickles, 27
tips, 25
pies
All-Butter Pie Dough, 71
Appalachian Pumpkin Pie, 161
Green Tomato Pie, 158
Mock Apple Pie, 157
Vodka Pie Dough, 72
pineapple
Pineapple Pound Cake, 162
Pineapple Upside-Down Cake, 154
Punch for 50, 143
Triple-Layer Carrot Cake, 150
pork and beans: Mick's Baked Beans, 114
pork loin: Pennies, Dollars, and Gold Potpie, 99–100
potatoes
Golden Potato Salad, 109
Pennies, Dollars, and Gold Potpie, 99–100
potpie: Pennies, Dollars, and Gold Potpie, 99–100
pudding: Mick's Banana Pudding, 176
pumpkin puree: Appalachian Pumpkin Pie, 161
punch: Punch for 50, 143

R

rolls. *See also* biscuits; breads
Grandmaw's Pepperoni Rolls, 127, 128
Grandmaw's Refrigerator Rolls, 56
Mary's Butter Rolls, 59
rum: Christmas Eve Eggnog, 140

S

salads
Coleslaw, 110
Golden Potato Salad, 109
Marinated Bean Salad, 113
Spring Salad Dressing, 80
saltine crackers
Appalachian Skillet Cornbread Dressing, 117
Mom's Meatloaf, 87
sauces
Grandmaw's West Virginia Hot Dog Chili Sauce, 78
Homemade Applesauce, 77
Oyster Mushroom Sauce, 81
Quick Cherry Sauce, 77
sausage
Sausage Balls, 131
Sausage Patties with Gravy, 49
scallions
Grandmaw's Baked Squash, 118
Marinated Bean Salad, 113
sherbert: Punch for 50, 143
sorghum: Appalachian Pumpkin Pie, 161
sour cream: Bacon Spinach Artichoke Dip, 132
spinach: Bacon Spinach Artichoke Dip, 132
squash
Garden Medley Pickles, 29
Grandmaw's Baked Squash, 118
Squash Pickles, 27

T

tea: Sweet Tea, 139
tomatoes
Grandmaw's West Virginia Hot Dog Chili Sauce, 78
Green Tomato Onion Cornbread, 64
Green Tomato Pickles, 30
Green Tomato Pie, 158
Mom's Meatloaf, 87
Sloppy Joes, 97
Toms Brook Volunteer Fire Department, 92–93
turkey
Appalachian Skillet Cornbread Dressing, 117
Roast Turkey, 84

V

vanilla wafers: Mick's Banana Pudding, 176
vodka: Vodka Pie Dough, 72

W

wax beans: Marinated Bean Salad, 113
West Virginia Day, 127
white chocolate: Triple-Chocolate Hot Cocoa Mix, 144
Worcestershire sauce
Dad's BBQ Chicken, 94
Mom's Meatloaf, 87
Sloppy Joes, 97

Y

yeast
Grandmaw's Refrigerator Rolls, 56–57
Mary's Butter Rolls, 59
tips, 55

Z

zucchini
Garden Medley Pickles, 29
Mock Apple Pie, 157
Zucchini Bread, 153